THE HONOR OF COMMAND

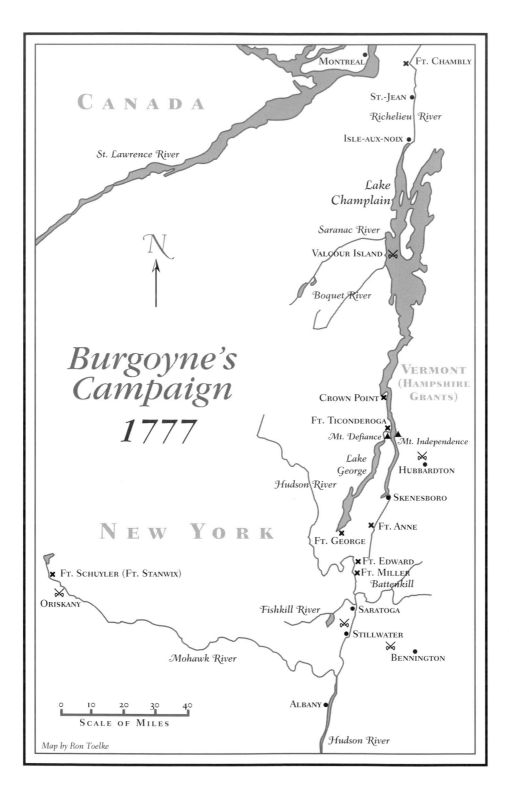

Burgoyne's Campaign 1777

CANADA

MONTREAL

FT. CHAMBLY

ST.-JEAN

Richelieu River

ISLE-AUX-NOIX

St. Lawrence River

N

Lake Champlain

Saranac River

VALCOUR ISLAND

Boquet River

VERMONT (HAMPSHIRE GRANTS)

CROWN POINT

FT. TICONDEROGA

Mt. Defiance

Mt. Independence

Lake George

HUBBARDTON

Hudson River

SKENESBORO

NEW YORK

FT. ANNE

FT. GEORGE

FT. SCHUYLER (FT. STANWIX)

FT. EDWARD

FT. MILLER

ORISKANY

Battenkill

Fishkill River

SARATOGA

STILLWATER

Mohawk River

BENNINGTON

SCALE OF MILES

0   10   20   30   40

ALBANY

Hudson River

Map by Ron Toelke

The strategic Lake Champlain–Hudson valley corridor in 1777

THE HONOR OF COMMAND

GENERAL BURGOYNE'S SARATOGA CAMPAIGN

STUART MURRAY

Images from the Past
Bennington, Vermont

Cover: Contemporary rebel artist John Trumbull commemorated the surrender ceremonies with this painting of John Burgoyne as he offers his sword to Horatio Gates after the defeat of the British Army in the Saratoga Campaign of 1777.

1 2 3 4 5 6 7 8 9 10 XXX 04 03 02 01 00 99 99 98 97

Library of Congress Cataloging-in-Publication Data
Murray, Stuart, 1948–
    The honor of command: General Burgoyne's Saratoga campaign, June–October
    1777/by Stuart Murray.
        p.   cm.
    Includes bibliographical references (p.   ) and index.
    ISBN 1-884592-03-1 (paper)
    1. Saratoga Campaign, 1777.   2. Burgoyne, John, 1722–1792.   3. United States—
    History—Revolution, 1775-1783—British forces.   I. Title.
E241.S2M87   1998
973.3'41—dc21   97-25356
                                                          CIP

Copyright© 1998 Images from the Past, Inc.
Tordis Ilg Isselhardt, Publisher

Printed in the United States of America

Text: Adobe Garamond
Display: Castellar MT
Ornaments: Rococo Ornaments MT
Paper: 70 lb. Fortune Matte
Cover: 12pt C1S
Design and Composition: Macintosh
    8100/80, with 172mb RAM, Quark
    XPress 3.32, Adobe Photoshop 3.0,
    Adobe Illustrator 5.5

Production: Open Press Interface between
    Stillwater Studio, Stillwater NY, and
    Thomson-Shore, Inc., Dexter MI
Scanner: Magitex 1875
Imagesetter: Purup Magnum
Press: (text) 40" Heidelberg Speedmaster ZP,
    (cover) 40" Heidelberg 501H-4C SM74
Printer: Thomson-Shore, Inc., Dexter MI
Cover Films: M&J Prepress, Albany NY

My rank only serves to place me in a motionless, drowsy, irksome medium, or rather vacuum, too low for the honor of command. . . .

Major General John Burgoyne, writing in 1776 from Boston, where he was a staff officer under General Gage.

DEDICATION

To the re-enactors

CONTENTS

The army embarks tomorrow, to approach the Enemy. We are to contend for the King and the constitution of Great Britain, to vindicate Law, and to relieve the oppressed. . . .

Major General John Burgoyne
Address to his troops, 1777

Led on by lust of lucre and renown,
Burgoyne came marching with his thousands down;
High were his thoughts and furious his career;
Puff'd with self-confidence and pride severe;
Swoll'n with the idea of his future deeds,
Onward to ruin each advantage leads.

Philip Freneau
From a 1778 poem by this popular rebel writer

PREFACE

This is the story of General John Burgoyne's doomed Saratoga campaign in 1777, told briefly, and from his perspective, set where the British commander headquartered, marched, and fought.

There are many longer histories of the crucial Saratoga campaign, and they often disagree about the facts, as do various memoirs. This book is based both on original documents and secondary sources, but there are some assumptions made—all of them grounded on ten years of research and writing about the Revolutionary period. Chapter notes address some of the controversial points and explain why the author chose one so-called fact over another.

If this book can bring to life the memory of the courageous royal army that struggled and lost in the Saratoga campaign, then it will have contributed some small part to the dynamic legacy of the American Revolution.

Stuart Murray
East Chatham, New York

By the time Sir Joshua Reynolds painted this portrait of him in 1767, Colonel John Burgoyne had won the admiration of King George III by raising a crack regiment of light dragoons.

INTRODUCTION

For decades afterwards, the people of the frontiers called 1777 "The Year of the Bloody Sevens," a time of fear, death, and destruction, as the British government tried to stamp out the rebellion in its American colonies.

That spring, a royal army invaded from the north, through the Lake Champlain-Hudson River corridor, while another advanced eastward, along the Mohawk Valley. Both aimed for Albany. British Redcoats and German auxiliaries fought alongside colonial loyalists and Indians, capturing fortresses, attacking rebel settlements and farms, driving their enemies before them.

At the head of the northern British army, Major General John Burgoyne was determined to be the one who saved the tottering empire in America. At first, it appeared Burgoyne would have his triumph, as he battled his way to the Hudson River. Yet, all that summer, the stubborn rebels fought back, slowing his advance, inflicting irreplaceable losses, and defeating the Mohawk Valley invaders.

When September came, Burgoyne found himself harried by overwhelming numbers on every side, his supply line threatened, and no hope of reinforcement. The road to Albany was blocked at Saratoga by a rebel force twice as large as Burgoyne's, but for a man of his ambition, retreat was out of the question. He chose to attack.

John Burgoyne's defeat and the surrender at Saratoga on October 17, 1777, became the turning point in the American Revolution.

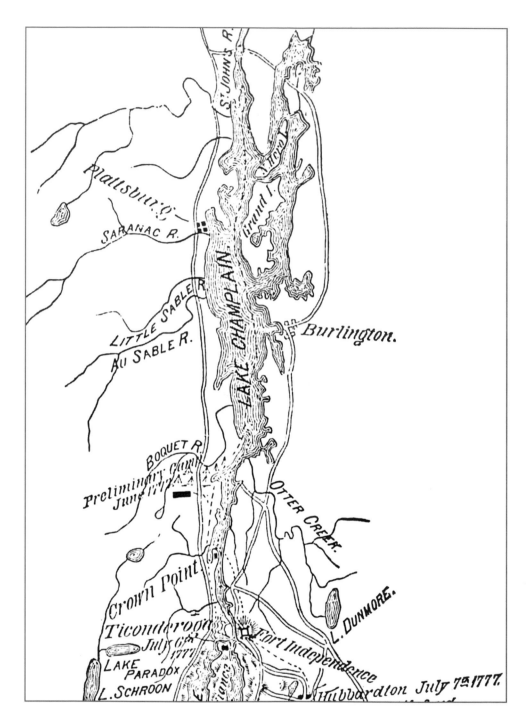

Burgoyne's advance over Lake Champlain led southward to forts Crown
Point and Ticonderoga, following the invasion route of 1776, when the
British had defeated a rebel fleet at the battle at Valcour Island before
being forced by cold weather to withdraw back to Canada.

St.-Jean, Quebec

June 13, 1777

At sunrise on this brilliant spring morning, the northern army of King George III assembled at the Richelieu River, ready to strike a decisive blow against the rebellion in the American colonies.

On the shores of the mud-brown river were eight thousand regulars, a thousand loyalist volunteers and workmen, and four hundred Indians. They lined up at the water's edge on docks and beaches, waited in rank on parade grounds and boatyards, and crowded through narrow streets between the whitewashed houses in the garrison town of St.-Jean-sur-Richelieu.

In grimy tent villages back from the waterfront, several hundred women and children—British, American, and German families of the soldiers—packed up their few belongings to follow the army. At the officers' quarters, elegant ladies scurried their servants here and there, loading luggage into two-wheeled calashes to be put aboard ship. Just like the impoverished families of ordinary soldiers, these women would share the dangers of the coming campaign.

Snare drums rattled and noncoms shouted orders as the fighting men filed onto schooners and sloops, gunboats and whaleboats; they crammed the thwarts of flat-bottomed bateaux and sat singly in bark canoes paddled by Indians and French-Canadians. Five hundred bateaux were packed with the troops of seven British regiments in scarlet and five German regiments—most hired from the princes of Brunswick and Hesse—in coats of green or blue.

The king's Northern Army mounted the invasion from staging areas on the Richelieu River, such as this one at St.-Jean, where warships and transports are pictured.

The boats proceeded upstream toward Lake Champlain, as the sun climbed over low-lying islands and forested shoreline. On the open water, the flotilla formed up in four columns, following regimental flags that fluttered gaily in the breeze. Men sang and bands played as sunlight glinted on the polished brass of uniform and cannon and sparkled on the blades of a thousand oars. The lake rippled with a fresh breeze that filled the sails of trim warships manned by sailors and officers of the Royal Navy. Some ships had been built last year at St.-Jean's yards, others fabricated in England and brought across the sea in sections that were hauled up the Richelieu for reassembly. They were swift, powerfully armed, and the rebels had nothing to match them.

The fleet's largest was the *Inflexible*, a three-masted sloop-of-war with twenty guns, accompanied by the schooners *Lady Maria* and *Carleton*. The schooner *Royal George* and its twenty-four cannon had been captured last autumn after the total defeat of the rebel squadron on Champlain, and several other good prizes had been taken in the victory. Twenty fast gunboats mounted swivel cannon in their bows, and the square-nosed radeau *Thunderer* carried heavy mortars for blasting apart rebel defensive works.

The men marveled at the beauty of water and forest all around. Most of them had been in America only a year, brought over to drive the rebel invaders from Canada. Last summer these troops had pursued the retreating enemy all the way up Lake Champlain, but their advance had been slowed by stiffening rebel resistance, and at last stopped by the coming of cold weather. Quartered all winter in private homes and barracks, the troops now were eager to resume their conquest, this time all the way to New York City if need be. Reinforced by more good regiments this spring, they were as splendid a fighting machine as any in the world, and the rank and file knew it.

Certainly, this was the greatest flotilla ever to pass through the natural corridor that for more than a century and a half had been a battleground for the warring colonies of Britain and France. The invasion route led from Montreal southward through the Champlain Valley, between the Adirondack Mountains to the west and the Green Mountains to the east. Fifteen years earlier, the British had conquered French Canada and brought peace to this blood-soaked country. Then, in 1775, the English-speaking colonies had risen against the crown, and fighting resumed.

This expedition was to capture Lake Champlain, then Lake George, and advance to the Hudson River and the city of Albany. It was the opinion of the British high command—generals, politicians, and King George himself—that when it joined with another royal army advancing northward from New York, the rebellion would be doomed. The ultimate success of the campaign lay upon the shoulders of a man who was both a general and a politician, and also a favorite of the king: Major General John Burgoyne.

As his army sailed up the lake, General Burgoyne stood in the bow of a pinnace, reviewing each regiment. In full sight of the troops, he held his plumed tricorne aloft to salute the royal colors flying from the mast of the *Lady Maria*, his flagship.

Gallant soldier, well-connected courtier, a tall and handsome man-about-London Town, Burgoyne was considered an able playwright and a less able gambler at cards and horses. An elected member of the British House of Commons, he was also colonel and founder of the Queen's 16th Light Dragoons. As he posed in his smallboat this glorious spring morning, the general was eager to win a resounding triumph on this campaign, for that would make him one of the most important men in the British Empire.

Many of Burgoyne's troops were just as eager to whip the rebels. A desire for revenge seethed in the embittered loyalists, who had been driven from their homes by the rebels and threatened with death if they returned. Also in the expedition were men of the 29th Regiment of Foot, whose fellow soldiers had been accused of causing the "Boston Massacre" in 1770. The 47th Foot, too, had reason to hate the rebels, for they had been bloodied in 1775 at the battle of Bunker Hill.

As a staff officer at Boston then, Burgoyne had watched the regulars attack rebel entrenchments on Breed's Hill again and again, only to be mowed down by point-blank musketry. He grudgingly conceded that the rebels had stood up to those bayonet charges, but he pointed out that they had possessed the advantage of firing from earthworks.

Burgoyne had only contempt for the fighting ability of the American soldier in the field. He did not take seriously the opinion of his former 16th Dragoons subordinate, Charles Lee, now a rebel officer, who believed the best of the Americans were as good as any light infantry in the world. Even after Bunker Hill, Burgoyne considered the rebels no more than "a rabble in arms." In the open, in what he called "a fair fight," no untrained rebels would dare hold their ground against the ferocious assault of the British infantryman. He said "the onset of Bayonets in the hands of the Valiant is irresistible." He intended to drive the rebels out of their defenses by bombarding them with artillery fire.

There were those who thought he had brought too much artillery along on this campaign, but he believed his one hundred and thirty-eight guns would be needed to reduce rebel-held Fort Ticonderoga, which stood a hundred miles up Lake Champlain, barring the way. There, during the French and Indian War, repeated British frontal assaults unsupported by artillery had been shattered, resulting in a bloody defeat.

Burgoyne would not frontally attack Ticonderoga, known as the "Gibraltar of America." Instead, he would blow the defenses to bits, just as the artillery he had commanded at the battle of Bunker Hill had shelled rebel-held Charlestown and set it ablaze. Overwhelming firepower would crack the rebel defenses at Ticonderoga, which was on the west side of the lake, and do the same to the new defensive works the rebels were building on Mount Independence across a strategic narrows. Burgoyne would hammer the rebels into surrender—those who were not yet cowed by the threat of his Indians.

Scattered in loose formation in the vanguard of the flotilla were scores of light canoes filled with the warriors of more than a dozen nations. Some were from the Iroquois and Algonquin peoples of Quebec and the Mohawk Valley, but the majority had been recruited from the western wilderness of the Great Lakes and the Ohio. The eastern nations lived for the most part in cabins and farming communities and for generations had traded with whites and fought alongside and against them. They knew the whites well. The western peoples, however, were strangers in this country. Some, like the Ottawas and Chippewas, had fought for the French in the last war. Others, like the Sioux, Sac, Fox, and Winnebagoes, had seldom before been east of Fort Detroit.

These tribes well remembered how Chief Pontiac of the Ottawas had led a rebellion in 1763, besieged Detroit, and captured several British frontier posts before he made peace. Now, the warriors of the West had come to fight for Burgoyne, who promised they again would win the honors of war and carry home plunder and scalps.

A contemporary German artist's view of a French-Canadian farmer.

In company with the Indians, and leading them, were French-Canadian frontiersmen who had won their reputations by fighting against the British Army. The *Canadien* scouts and Indians would be difficult to manage, but Burgoyne considered them essential for ambushing enemy patrols and taking prisoners for interrogation. More than that, the very rumor of French and Indian war parties would strike terror into the rebel militias, who would flee from the path of his army. It was true that Burgoyne and the

British high command had been denounced by members of Parliament for employing Indians. Certainly, there was fear among veteran officers that the Indians would massacre settlers, rebel or loyalist.

Yet, even though Burgoyne had never campaigned with or against Indians before, he was sure he could make them obey the rules of civilized war-making. The general was a very confident man.

At fifty-four, John Burgoyne was at the height of his powers, admired by royalty and commoner alike as a dashing example of all that was best in the English ruling class. Sometimes called "Gentlemanly Johnny," Burgoyne was admired by his troops, who liked his exquisite good manners and his flair for elegant clothes. They also respected his genuine consideration for the welfare of his men, a trait not often found in high-ranking British officers.

In his youth, he had won fame leading horsemen against the French and Spanish in some minor European skirmishes, but he had not taken part in the French and Indian War and, so, was inexperienced in American warfare. That inexperience did not deter Burgoyne from making a plan to defeat the rebellion in the northern colonies. On a trip home to England last winter, he had presented the scheme to Lord George Germain, colonial secretary, who submitted it to King George. Burgoyne's strategy called for three simultaneous thrusts, all meeting at Albany, where the east-flowing Mohawk River joined the south-flowing Hudson. A force of regulars, loyalists, and Indians would advance eastward along the Mohawk, and the British army in New York City would attack up the Hudson. These would converge on Albany, where Burgoyne's force from Canada would unite with them both.

The general had been so persuasive that Germain and the king appointed him commander of the northern army—a post he wanted all along. This appointment was an affront to Canada's governor-general, Guy Carleton, an able commander who had won distinction in the French and Indian War. In 1775, Carleton had defended Canada against the rebel in-

As a young man, the rakish Burgoyne was popular at the royal court and at the gaming tables.

J. Chapman sc.

vasion, and last fall had driven the enemy back up Lake Champlain to Ticonderoga. Burgoyne, who had been second-in-command then, considered Carleton much too cautious. The rebels had built a fleet of warships on the lake, and that had forced Carleton to build his own fleet and defeat the rebel ships. This had slowed the advance so long that cold weather set in, compelling the British to withdraw to Canada instead of assaulting Ticonderoga.

Burgoyne believed he would do better than Carleton. Time was short, however. He could not allow the sort of delays that had turned back Carleton. First, Ticonderoga must fall after only a short siege, prosecuted with

A contemporary American illustration honors the rebel fleet led by Benedict Arnold against the British on Lake Champlain in 1776—several vessels of which were captured and used by Burgoyne's army.

Fort Chambly, on the Richelieu River, was a strongpoint that changed hands in the early months of the Revolution.

a heavy bombardment. Next, the loyalists must join him and offer supplies as well as manpower. The appearance of so powerful a British force was expected to rally thousands of provincials who opposed the rebels and Congress. The support of armed loyalists was essential to intimidate rebel militias before they massed to fight him.

Burgoyne was especially concerned about the enemy firing from the cover of trees and rocks, the way they had defeated the regulars at Lexington and Concord. To counter these tactics, his troops had been trained in company-sized formations that could operate independently in rough, forested country like the terrain they would pass through. American militia also were known for their ability to throw up earthworks with amazing speed. It was from hastily dug earthworks at Breed's Hill that the rebels had killed so many of the general's friends and fellow officers.

Burgoyne was determined that after Ticonderoga fell, the decisive fighting of this campaign would be in the open field, where regulars could maneuver in disciplined, close ranks. Once the Indians drove the rebels from the cover of the woods, and his artillery smashed enemy earthworks apart like anthills, the bayonet would make quick work of them.

There were those in the government and military who said Burgoyne's force should instead have been sent to unite with the larger army in New

York City and help capture the middle colonies. Why attempt to force the Champlain Valley, where Fort Ticonderoga stood in the way? Ticonderoga and four hundred miles of country in open rebellion. One reason was that King George opposed leaving Canada weakly defended, exposed to another rebel invasion. As for Burgoyne, he did not want to be subordinate to any other general. In sole command of this army, fighting for the very survival of the British Empire, was exactly where John Burgoyne, soldier and statesman, wanted to be. His steadily rising career had brought him to this moment, and he knew what had to be done and how to do it.

By now, Colonial Secretary Germain must have ordered Sir William Howe, who commanded in New York City, to begin his advance up the Hudson toward Albany. It had been disconcerting to hear from Carleton recently that Howe wanted instead to go southward to capture Philadelphia. Burgoyne assumed that Germain's orders to advance on Albany had not arrived in New York when Howe wrote Carleton about his plans.

As Burgoyne watched the army sailing past, bands playing, men cheering him in English and in German, he might have recalled his confident wager with Charles James Fox, a longtime friend in Commons. Burgoyne had bet fifty guineas that he would "be home victorious from America by Christmas Day, 1777."

Fox had taken the bet, then said disarmingly, "I believe when next you return to England you will be a prisoner on parole."

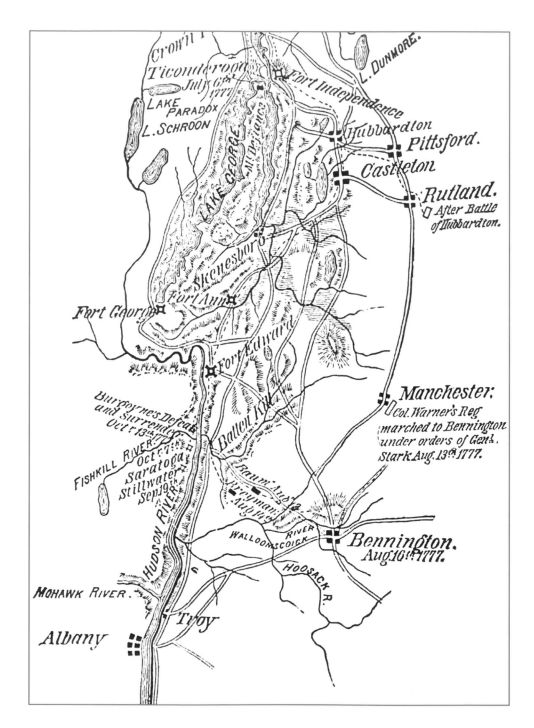

After capturing Crown Point and Ticonderoga, Burgoyne planned to advance over Lake George to the Hudson Valley.

THE FALLS
OF THE BOQUET RIVER

JUNE 21, 1777

Everything went well as Burgoyne's army moved in four brigades, each making camp at twenty-mile intervals. The following brigade took over the campsite left by the brigade ahead, and the advance up the lake was efficient and steady.

The expedition's first main base was on the west side of Champlain at Cumberland Head. After off-loading troops and equipment here, most of the larger vessels returned to St.-Jean to pick up artillery, thousands of kegs of gunpowder and rum, barrels, bales, and crates of supplies and personal belongings. The ships also boarded families, camp followers, and merchants, who would remain at the rear of the army throughout the campaign. (The women and children had their own encampments near the troops.) Several vessels towed sections of a pontoon bridge especially designed to link both sides of the lake at narrows. Later, this bridge would be carted overland to the Hudson River for the army to cross on the final march to Albany.

The mountains on both sides of Champlain were becoming steeper. In the years since the end of the French and Indian War new farms had been cleared in this virgin forest, and increasing numbers of settlers were populating the eastern country called the Hampshire Grants—lately termed Vermont by those who would have the region repudiate the dual claims of New

With oar and sail, Burgoyne's army advanced unchallenged along
the wild and beautiful shores of Lake Champlain.

Hampshire and New York. In the past this country had been a no-man's-
land between hostile French and English settlements, but now there were
budding hamlets along the shorelines. These had been abandoned recently
for fear of Burgoyne's Indians. No matter whether the inhabitants were
loyal or rebel, they believed they were in danger.

Loyal Americans were not at risk as far as Burgoyne was concerned,
however, for his Indian fighters had remained under control. After giving
them a speech today, he would send the Indians out to find the rebel forces
commanded by General Philip Schuyler of Albany, and report back on
their strength.

Burgoyne had come halfway up the lake, and in a day or so his advance brigade would be at Crown Point, the first fort held by the rebels. The battle was at hand.

Late in the afternoon, Burgoyne went over the side of the *Lady Maria* and down a rope ladder to his pinnace for the short trip up the Boquet River to the Indian camp. He was resplendent in his scarlet and white uniform with its gold lacing, the better to impress the warriors, who had to be told exactly what he required of their behavior in the field. They would be allowed to fight in their own way, but there must be no hostilities against innocents or loyalists. He would pay for the scalps of enemy soldiers, but would pay more for prisoners. After all, he was a man of honor and mercy, who intended to defeat the rebels, not massacre them. He had composed a proclamation to the provincials, warning them either to remain out of the fighting or rally to his side.

Anyone who opposed him in a "Phrenzy of Hostility" was warned that he would "stand acquitted in the eyes of God and men in denouncing and executing the vengeance of the state against the willful outcast. The messengers of justice and wrath await them in the field. . . ." Those messengers of wrath were at hand in the camp of painted warriors. The legendary stealthy Indian fighter was the nightmare of white settlers, and fear of Indian kidnappers haunted children from Fort Pitt to London, Fort Detroit to Paris.

Two miles up the narrow river, Burgoyne's pinnace put ashore and he was met by British and German officers who led him along a footpath to the Indian camp. The warriors were seated around a central council fire, and Burgoyne joined the senior chiefs and elders in the inner circle, the place of honor. In their finest furs and feathers, trinkets, beads, and trade blankets, they waited soberly for the general to rise and speak. After an appropriately long silence, he stood and addressed them in flattering and flowery language, calling them "too sagacious and too faithful" ever to be won over by the treachery of the rebels. The speech was translated in several tongues as Burgoyne indulged in his natural tendency toward grandiloquent prose. At his most florid expressions of praise, the Indians clamored in assent, for they admired such eloquence.

Burgoyne accused the rebels of abusing the mercy and clemency of the "great King, our common father," and waxed ever more passionate: "Warriors, you are free—go forth in the might and valour of your cause—strike at the common enemies of Great Britain and America, disturbers of public order, peace, and happiness, destroyers of commerce, parricides of state." He indicated the other officers around him, saying they "esteem you as brothers in the war; emulous in glory and in friendship, we will endeavour reciprocally to give and to receive examples . . . and we will strive to imitate your perseverance in enterprise, and your constancy to resist hunger, weariness, and pain."

The general then laid out his terms for their conduct in the coming fight, saying "the dictates of our religion" required warriors to "regulate your passions when they overbear," and admonished that "it is nobler to spare than to revenge." He explained: "The King has many faithful subjects dispersed in the provinces; consequently you have many brothers there." He commended the Indians' "magnanimity of character" and demanded their "most serious attention to the rules," specifically: "I positively forbid blood-

This stylized nineteenth-century illustration pictures the council on the Boquet River before the fighting began, when Burgoyne told his Indian allies they must obey the rules of honorable warfare and not kill the wounded or attack innocents.

shed when you are not opposed in arms. Aged men, women and children, and prisoners must be held sacred from the knife or hatchet, even in time of actual conflict."

They were told to refrain from their usual practice of killing enemy wounded. Nor were the wounded to be scalped, not even if they were dying, "and still less pardonable, if possible, will it be held to kill men in that condition" in order to be justified in taking scalps only from the dead.

As he spoke, Burgoyne faced hundreds of fighters who had spent a lifetime scalping and killing the likes of him and their so-called loyalist "brothers in the provinces." Many of these warriors and their forefathers had grown up hating the British colonists, whom they called "Bostonians," and the defeat of Pontiac's Rebellion still stung. They had not joined this campaign to defend the honor of King George, who claimed to be their "Great Father Across the Sea," but for scalps and plunder.

When Burgoyne sat down, one of the old Iroquois chiefs rose to reply with language almost as flowery. "We have been tried and tempted by the Bostonians, but we have loved our father [King George], and our hatchets have been sharpened upon our affections. . . . With one common assent we promise a constant obedience to all you have ordered, and all you shall order; and may the Father of Days give you many, and success."

When the speaker was finished, there was a shout of approval, and Burgoyne bowed in reply. Then he and his entourage withdrew just as kegs of rum from his flagship were rolled in to be tapped for the night's war dance. The other officers did not stay to watch. Serving Indians rum and encouraging them to attack whites deeply troubled those in the army who had seen the devastation caused by war parties on the frontiers.

The Indians drank and danced for hours, their blood-curdling shrieks carrying across the Boquet River to the nearby white encampments. Through the night, the drums and shouting of the war dance could be heard in the general's cabin aboard the *Lady Maria*, riding at anchor in Cumberland Bay. By morning, all was silent. The warriors were gone, scattered in dozens of bands ranging south and west, seeking the enemy.

In the name of King George III, John Burgoyne had loosed the Indian fighters, and there was no guarantee he could call them back.

On June 30, Burgoyne issued a general order: "The army embarks tomorrow, to approach the Enemy. We are to contend for the King, and the constitution of Great Britain, to vindicate Law, and to relieve the oppressed—a cause in which his Majesty's Troops and those of the Princes his Allies, will feel equal excitement. The Services required of this particular expedition are critical and conspicuous. During our progress occasions may occur in which, nor difficulty, nor labour, nor Life are to be regarded. This Army must not Retreat."

A Scottish Highland light infantryman.

The force could not yet depart, however, for a rainstorm swept the lake for three days, upsetting bateaux, ruining campsites, blowing down tents, and soaking firewood so that the troops could scarcely get a cooked meal. The advance was held up until the weather broke, and then it turned hot and muggy, with swarms of stinging blackflies that descended on the army like a curse. Summer heat settled over the Champlain Valley, and the army experienced the mighty hardships of weather, terrain, and distance that so many European soldiers had met in American campaigns.

The soldiers' uniform and gear were heavy, together weighing as much as sixty pounds, but so far there were boats and ships to carry them. The army's daily routine required gathering wood and water, working in fatigue parties to drain campsites and dig latrines, tenting and striking, drilling and parading, cleaning equipment, repairing boats, arguing and fighting, enduring harsh discipline, and putting up with arrogant gentleman officers often no more than boys.

It seemed that with every mile the army advanced into enemy territory, the beautiful country all around became ever more unfamiliar, ever more threatening. Heat, rain, blackflies, and humidity made it worse. Then came the unexpected good news that Crown Point had been abandoned without a fight by the rebels, who had fallen back on Fort Ti and Mount Independence. There were fewer than twenty-five hundred rebels in all, not enough to garrison the works at Ticonderoga and Mount Independence, which required at least ten thousand men to withstand a prolonged siege. Burgoyne was grateful not to have to fight for Crown Point, and he hoped he would not need to besiege Fort Ticonderoga for long.

Hundreds of boats of all shapes and sizes carried Burgoyne's army over
Lake Champlain on its way to attack forts Crown Point and Ticonderoga.

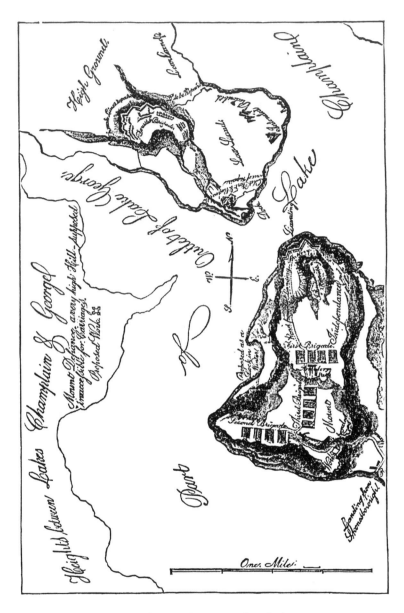

By 1777, the rebels had created a strong fortified encampment on Mount Independence, across from Fort Ticonderoga, both shown in the contemporary map by artist John Trumbull.

CROWN POINT, TICONDEROGA, AND MOUNT INDEPENDENCE

JULY 1, 1777

Burgoyne's army pushed southward to occupy Crown Point, where the military stores for the assault on Ticonderoga and Mount Independence would be assembled. The commander established his headquarters in Crown Point, once a grand fort, but which had suffered from fifteen years of neglect and then from fire and accidental explosions four years ago. Coming from the north, here was the first narrowing of Lake Champlain, only half a mile wide, with the heights above Ticonderoga visible twelve miles away to the south.

Near Crown Point stood the dilapidated walls of Fort St. Frederick, the original French bastion, built in the 1730s and blown up when abandoned in 1759. That year, the British had begun to erect, at great expense, the new fortress they called Crown Point, its ramparts twenty-five feet thick, the outer ditches carved into native limestone. In the years since the French wars, however, the fort had been poorly maintained, and the approach of Burgoyne's army had convinced the rebels it was wiser to withdraw.

Now began Burgoyne's maneuvers to advance on Ticonderoga and Mount Independence. Germans and Indians moved to camps along Lake

Champlain's east shore; British and loyalists took positions on the western side. The army was arrayed on hillsides and beaches, on ridges and in stream outlets, and it was a spectacular, inspiring sight.

From Crown Point at night, Burgoyne could look along the shorelines and see hundreds of campfires twinkling against the dark of hills and lake. Watch lights of anchored warships bobbed in the night, and guard boats passed back and forth on patrol, the lamps on their mastheads swaying as they went from ship to shore, past campsite and fortress. Across the lake, on

View of Ticonderoga from Mount Independence, with the British ship *Inflexible* at left, and the water route northward to Crown Point at right; this 1777 drawing was made on the spot by Lieutenant H. Rudyard of the royal engineers.

the gravel shoreline of Button Mold Bay, the army's civilian followers had arrived in hundreds of boats to make their noisy encampment and await the outcome of the approaching battle.

The music of brass bands rose from docks nearby, and the songs of soldiers in their scattered campsites drifted on the breeze. From somewhere hearty laughter rang out, echoing across the water, a cheerful sound in the summer night.

A nineteenth-century view of the remains of Crown Point.

At Crown Point, Burgoyne and his staff planned the capture of Ticonderoga and Mount Independence.

Second-in-command was the Englishman Major General William Phillips, an excellent artillery officer. Commanding the advance corps was Brigadier General Simon Fraser, a Scot who had spent much of his military career in America. In European battles against the French, he had been a comrade of both Phillips and Major General Friedrich von Riedesel, who led the German forces and was third in command.

A Brunswicker, Baron Riedesel longed to acquire horses for his two hundred dragoons, who had taken ship from home without their mounts. Horses too often died on ocean journeys, so they had not been transported to America. Since horses were scarce in Canada, the dragoons would have to get them by raiding rebel farms and villages. Until then, the Brunswick dragoons replaced their high riding boots with infantry footwear and wore military-style cocked hats instead of their dashing plumed hats, but they still carried three-foot cavalry sabers and short muskets.

Though openly critical of Burgoyne's arrogance, Baron Friedrich von Riedesel, commander of the German auxiliaries, was a dependable and able veteran officer.

Himself a veteran dragoon, Riedesel was eager to lead his regiment on horseback into the rolling country of the Hudson River. With foresight, he had trained his men in wilderness tactics, making them use the shelter of trees when firing and loading. He also required his company of Brunswick *Jaegers*—"hunters," as these riflemen were called—to improve their marksmanship in an effort to match the long-range threat from rebel riflemen.

Many of Burgoyne's provincial volunteers were good with the rifle. Led by Lieutenant Colonel John Peters, who commanded the largest of four units, they were called the Queen's Loyal Rangers. Most had been recruited from New York, and others were from the Hampshire Grants, where Peters had lived before the war. The rangers were commonly known as Peters Corps and numbered almost three hundred men, all unswervingly set against the rebels and Congress. A lawyer and a native of Connecticut, Peters was a graduate of Yale and had been sent by New York's Gloucester County (later part of southern Vermont) as a delegate to the Continental Congress in Philadelphia. He had objected to the Congress's plans for independence and as a result was set upon and beaten by the

Baroness Friederike von Riedesel followed her husband on the campaign, and also brought along their little children.

Sons of Liberty. After that, he swore to fight the rebels, even though he had to defy his own father, a staunch republican.

In addition to the few French-Canadian frontiersmen with the Indians, a hundred or so had been recruited as fighting men, formed into two companies. Another hundred and fifty *Canadiens* served mainly as hired boatmen and carters. Like most of their people, they had little enthusiasm for taking sides in this war.

Burgoyne's British troops were well trained, many recently stationed in Ireland and kept in a state of readiness for insurrection. Most of the German privates, on the other hand, were inexperienced soldiers, new conscripts, their regiments hurriedly (and often forcibly) raised by the rulers of Brunswick and Hanau—a vassal state of Hesse—who had contracted to send thousands of "auxiliaries" to fight for King George III.

The German officers, however, were mostly tough veteran campaigners, professionals who had proven themselves in European battles. The junior officers of the regular British regiments ranged from hard-bitten, aging lieutenants, who had no hope of further promotion, to callow ensigns—often the second and third sons of noble families—just starting their careers. In 1777, Burgoyne's campaign, with its promise of fame and glory, seemed an ideal place for an aspiring young hero.

Winning fame and glory was also foremost on General Burgoyne's mind just then. Ticonderoga would be his first test as commander of an army in the field, and capturing the fort and Mount Independence with their ten Continental regiments would clear the way to Albany.

Occasional firing echoed across the lake and through the ravines as Burgoyne's advance elements encountered rebel skirmishers and unsuspecting stragglers, but there were no major clashes.

Hessen Hanau Regt. Erbprinz.
1778.   F. v Germann
E. Sack

A German infantryman from Hanau.

The rebels, concentrated in fortifications on both sides of the lake, were under the experienced former British field officer Arthur St. Clair, another Scot who had seen much action in America. St. Clair had been reinforced to about four thousand men, but was still too short of troops to sally out and attack the British maneuvers, which went unopposed. At one point, Burgoyne wondered what it meant when the rebels fired thirteen cannon in slow succession. He learned from spies that George Washington had won a small clash in New Jersey, and the garrison was saluting the victory. This was no more than a minor distraction, though, for at that moment Riedesel's Germans were landing at Three Mile Point to begin their movement around the eastern defenses at Mount Independence. At the same time, Fraser was leading his brigade swiftly through the woods around the western outer works of Ticonderoga to cut off communication with Lake George.

Fraser occupied abandoned rebel defensive works on Mount Hope, west of the fort, and captured some pickets stationed in outlying posts. Soon, the strategic portage between lakes Champlain and George was in his hands, blocking that route from Ticonderoga. Meanwhile, Riedesel's troops, working their way toward Mount Independence on the east side of the lake, found their progress hampered by swamps and terrible heat. The Germans were blocked by East Creek, broader and deeper than they had expected, and their attempt to reach and cut off the only road eastward was slowed. In the swamps, they suffered from the stinging blackflies that swarmed about a man's head, causing swelling from the bites, making soldiers half mad.

By now, it appeared General St. Clair was prepared to withstand a siege. After Carleton's rebuff last year, Burgoyne dreaded being slowed down here, so the defenders must not hold out, lest Congress send more troops north, the militias rise and fight. St. Clair had to be shown his cause was hopeless.

Then, good reconnaissance found the vulnerability of the defensive works. Fraser's scouts clambered up Sugar Loaf, a steep height south of Ticonderoga and across the inlet to Ticonderoga Creek. From here, they looked down to see the fort lying exposed, within cannon shot. Even Mount Independence, on an elevation higher than Ticonderoga, was within range. If guns could be hauled up here, the fort was doomed. Looking on this, an Indian scout wondered aloud whether the "Great Father of the Sun" had just created this mountain, otherwise why in all these years of warfare had it never been occupied before? The answer was that most commanders did not think guns could be brought up those heights.

Ticonderoga was commanded by Mount Defiance, where Burgoyne's guns forced evacuation without the siege he had expected to lay.

On July 4, the first anniversary of the American Declaration of Independence, British artillerymen were digging out positions on Sugar Loaf while cannon were being dragged up the far slope. The next day, the first British gun appeared there, in sight of the rebels. Named Mount Defiance by the invaders, the position dominated Ticonderoga and also threatened the works at Mount Independence, where most of the rebel army was stationed. On that sprawling plateau were new-built cannon batteries and blockhouses, a hospital, barracks, lines of tents, and a central star fort of earth and timber. The rebels were still working on the unfinished defenses, which were linked to Ticonderoga by a floating bridge across the narrows. A little distance from the bridge, a log-and-chain boom prevented shipping and bateaux from entering the narrows between the rebel positions.

Rebel boats still could get from Ticonderoga and Mount Independence to Lake Champlain's South Bay and then sail south to Skenesboro, but the main rebel army could not escape in this direction, because St. Clair did not have enough vessels for all his soldiers. The noose of Burgoyne's advancing infantry tightened around the rebel defenders, and the only remaining escape route for the enemy was the track southeastward through the hamlet of Hubbardton. German troops struggled through the swamps by Mount Independence to cut that off.

By now, British stores were piling up at the Crown Point base, and officers' ladies arrived there along with supplies. So, too, did Burgoyne's personal baggage, including crates of wine, china, and silverware, and with all this came a French-Canadian woman he had taken as a mistress that spring.

Burgoyne was a widower, his wife having died a year ago. Though he was considered a ladies' man, Burgoyne had been faithful to Charlotte in the accepted manner of gentlemen of his day. Their marriage of twenty-two years had been a happy one in spite of his occasional affairs and bouts of wenching. As a young woman, Charlotte had accompanied him on European campaigns, but later became sickly and could not join him in America. Burgoyne had been on last year's aborted Ticonderoga campaign when his wife had died at home in England. (Their only child, a daughter, had died in 1764 at the age of ten.) He had been heartbroken at his wife's death, but lately he took comfort in his mistress, the wife of an ambitious supply contractor who did not complain.

The campaign was proceeding like clockwork. Burgoyne had taken Crown Point, and now mighty Ticonderoga, fabled in British and French military lore, was almost surrounded. It would have been more reassuring to him if some useful information had come in from the war parties, but other than reports of their ravaging and burning abandoned farms, he knew little of their whereabouts. Yet, as long as they were active and aggressive, keeping enemy scouts at bay, they would be valuable to him.

Then, early on the morning of July 6, Burgoyne was startled awake with the news that the rebels had fled in the night. Ticonderoga and Mount Independence were deserted. In a dispatch from abandoned Mount Independence, where he had joined Riedesel, Simon Fraser requested permission to pursue the enemy army eastward along the forest track to Hubbardton. Astonished and delighted, Burgoyne gave his approval, then sailed in the *Lady Maria* to Ticonderoga and Mount Independence. It was miraculous. The forts had been undamaged by the retreating rebels, who had left behind tons of stores and equipment.

The "Gibraltar of America" had fallen without a costly fight and without being blown up by the defenders. The great gray stone walls, cut and laid by Frenchmen twenty years earlier, loomed over the beautiful narrows of Lake Champlain, the heavy guns still pointing through the embrasures. Even the officers' quarters and barracks, stables, and storehouses were intact, as it was with most of the buildings on Mount Independence. Obviously, St. Clair cared more about a silent escape, saving his men to fight another day rather than demolishing his positions with explosions that would have warned Burgoyne and given him a chance to cut off retreat. Except for someone setting fire last night to a house on Mount Independence—alerting Fraser and Riedesel that something was happening—the enemy flight had been neatly carried out, their baggage and wounded sent by boat along South Bay, heading for Skenesboro.

The campaign was fast becoming the resounding triumph Burgoyne had hoped for, and he wasted no time savoring his first conquest. The log-and-chain boom was broken apart by a few close cannon shots, and the British flotilla sailed off to capture or destroy the fleeing rebel boats.

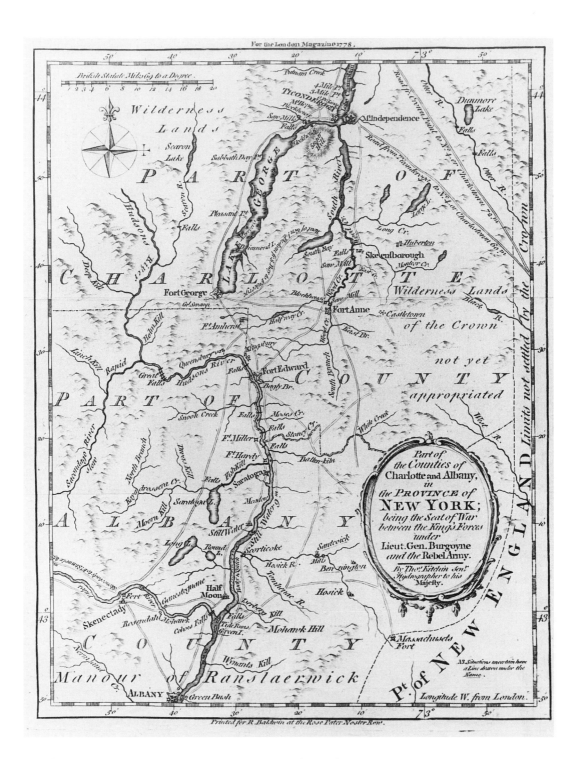

London Magazine titled this 1778 map "The Seat of War" between
the king's army and the rebels.

SKENESBORO AND FORT ANNE

JULY 10, 1777

Fortune seemed to be smiling on General John Burgoyne as he established his headquarters in the big yellow stone house of loyalist Philip Skene, founder of Skenesboro and a key advisor on the campaign. A retired career army officer, the Scottish-born Skene was proud to offer the general his grand home, which had been occupied by rebels ever since they forced his family from the estate two years earlier. This was a return in triumph for the loyalist, who insisted that many more like him soon would rally to Burgoyne's standards.

With the general to the manor house went thirty cartloads of gentlemanly accouterments, headquarters equipment and papers, and his mistress's ample baggage. Ironically, at the start of the campaign, Burgoyne had admonished his officers to take only what was absolutely essential. He had reminded them that in the last war, officers on campaign were known to sleep in common soldiers' tents and "often confined their baggage to a knapsack for months together."

Yet, one of the Brunswick officers observed that English gentlemen officers had their servants lug heavy portmanteaus full of clothes, "bags of hair powder, pomatum, cards, novels, and plays." Perhaps the Brunswicker was annoyed that Burgoyne saw fit at this time to write Riedesel a sharp letter criticizing the German officers for taking too much along.

Burgoyne lived up to his reputation as a gracious, generous host. Soldiers on guard duty at Skene's manor house heard the laughter of ladies and the guffaws of officers from the dining room, and when the singing began, Burgoyne took the lead. While the troops ate army-issue salt pork if they could not find fresh meat or poultry at the abandoned farms, the general's cooks often served his favorite delicacy: fresh rattlesnake soup.

The general had good reason to celebrate, for no one had expected his rapid advance. There had been sharp encounters here and there, and the rebels were working feverishly to destroy bridges and block roads, but they were too weak for a battle. True, the enemy had put up stiff resistance in fights with royal army detachments at Hubbardton to the east and at Fort Anne, south of Lake George, but the general attributed this to no more than the desperation of beaten troops trying to escape, not to their "gallant courage," as officers who had fought them had expressed it with a certain uneasiness. Even soldiers in the ranks were talking about the rebels standing firm and fighting hand-to-hand at Hubbardton.

Immediately after the fall of Ticonderoga, General Fraser had led a fast-moving force of mainly light infantry and grenadiers, pushing on through night and summer heat to surprise the American rear guard. Instead of turning tail, as expected, the enemy had fought back, their resistance fierce.

The rebels had done what a rear guard is supposed to do: slow down pursuers by making them deploy, then hold out as long as possible to give the main army time to get away. They had been mainly Massachusetts and New Hampshire Continentals led by Colonel Seth Warner, with some militia mixed in. At the height of the battle, in woods and on steep slopes, about a thousand men on both sides were engaged. The rebels had fought in good, rough order and held their ground when they might have run from British assaults.

Fraser actually found himself recoiling from a determined counterattack until Baron Riedesel arrived with reinforcements just in time to threaten the rebel flank. Only then did the enemy retreat, but even after melting into the forest, they kept taking deadly shots at the troops, with officers the prime targets. At least fifteen British and German officers were shot down, and in all, sixty rank and file died, almost a hundred and fifty wounded. It was a heavy loss, darkly reminiscent of the disasters at Lexington and Breed's Hill. The rebels had fewer killed and wounded—forty-one and ninety-six, respectively—but a couple of hundred were taken prisoner.

It was exceedingly strange for the British and German soldiers to see, up close, the motley New England regiments, especially the militia units, which included blacks and Indians, some very old men, and some small boys even younger than the greenest British ensigns. Burgoyne called Hubbard-ton a resounding victory, but the stories his troops told hung like a shadow over the army. Without doubt, the rebels had fought bravely.

It had been much the same, soon after, with the engagement near Fort Anne, though smaller in scale. Two hundred soldiers of the 9th Foot had hurried down the forest road from Skenesboro in search of fleeing rebels. The 9th's troops passed charred palisades of a fort burned by the enemy, and saw the boatyards at Wood Creek, where the rebels had built the vessels that had delayed Carleton last year. Soon, the Redcoats were slowed by fallen trees and destroyed bridges the enemy had left in their withdrawal. As the troops worked at clearing the road to Fort Anne, just a few miles ahead, they came under fire, and a battle began in the dense woods. After attack and counterattack, the Redcoats captured the flags of a New Hampshire Con-tinental regiment, but soon found themselves outflanked and suffering from sniper fire.

Up against New York militia as well as Continentals, the British were compelled to make a fighting withdrawal, even leaving their wounded be-hind, including an officer. After three hours, with a thunderstorm threat-ening to burst, the rebels still persistently harried the embattled Redcoats, who heard the distant thud and chop of axes felling more trees to block the road ahead. The British were almost surrounded, when a war whoop rang out, and another. Burgoyne's Indians were coming to the rescue. Soon, the rebels drifted away, their sniping ended. War whoops sounded ever closer until at last a British officer appeared, striding around a bend in the road, his scarlet coat tossed over one shoulder. When he saw his comrades, he leaned back and let out a war whoop, then began to laugh.

No Indians were there, but the enemy had fled.

The troops of the 9th Foot were unable to push on to attack Fort Anne, just as Fraser and Riedesel had not continued their pursuit after Hubbardton. The royal army had won both skirmishes, but the cost—especially in officers—had been dear. Moreover, the main body of the enemy army had escaped, and reinforcements were reportedly already gathering to the south. Burgoyne had to decide the campaign's next phase.

Would he return to Ticonderoga, as the original plan dictated, and sail his men down Lake George on boats transported over the portage from Champlain? In that direction lay the rebel-held Fort George, which would have to be taken. Or would he march through the forest south from Skenesboro, take Fort Anne, and attack the next post, Fort Edward, on the Hudson River?

This sawmill at Skenesboro turned out lumber for Arnold's hastily built fleet, which opposed the first British invasion in 1776.

Bateaux manned by French-Canadian boatmen transported much of Burgoyne's army and equipment.

Philip Skene urged the latter course, which required Burgoyne to build a military road from the manor at Skenesboro, through more than twenty miles of woods and swamplands and past Fort Anne. Skene proposed this even though General Schuyler's axemen were blocking the forest track from Skenesboro, flooding low ground, and destroying bridges. It would require much hard labor to repair what the rebels had ruined. Some believed Skene's real motive was to improve his own estate at royal expense, but by now there was justification in thinking the rebels would stoutly defend Fort George, which guarded the invasion route from Lake George to the Hudson. If, however, Burgoyne cut his way southward from Skenesboro, he would outflank Fort George and could capture it at will. Furthermore, he did not want to send his men back down South Bay to the portage at Ticonderoga. Moving backward would be bad for morale.

As the general pondered, there was much to be done to regroup his scattered army. The camp followers arrived, the women joining their men and caring for the scores of wounded and sick, many of whom had to be sent back to Montreal to recuperate. In spite of the unpredictability of his Indian allies and rumors of enemy reinforcements on the march, the campaign was going well. Even though the hired wagon drivers and laborers were too few, supply contractors inadequate, and only six hundred new loyalists had joined the force, he was ahead of schedule, with almost four months of campaigning weather left. More than ever, Riedesel's dragoons were appealing for a raid eastward to procure horses.

After a few days of deliberation, Burgoyne chose to take Skene's advice and build a road through the woods past Fort Anne. At the same time, the

Burgoyne decided against sending his army over Lake George,
which would have meant a retrograde movement from Skenesboro
instead of advancing steadily southward.

bulk of his heavy equipment, baggage, and supplies would be shipped by
water over Lake George, with a depot to be established at the southern
reaches of the lake.

The clever engineer, Lieutenant William Twiss, who had built the artillery road up the mountain that dominated Fort Ti, took charge of cross-
ing the swamplands, but it was more difficult than expected. At least forty
bridges and causeways had to be built, one of them two miles long. The
rebels had leveled everything in Burgoyne's path, abandoning and burning
Fort Anne, destroying military stores, cabins and barns, field and garden
crops. Only a charred waste was left in Burgoyne's path.

Although this was a bountiful country, virtually everything the men ate
had to be brought down from Canada at tremendous effort and cost.
Meanwhile, Riedesel urged a raid eastward to capture supplies, cattle, and
horses, so that the footsore Brunswick dragoons finally could be mounted
to serve as the excellent horsemen they were. Also, a move in force toward
the Hampshire Grants would hold New England troops there and keep
them from joining General Schuyler. First, however, Burgoyne had to get his
men clear of the entangling woods south of Skenesboro.

Day after day, loyalist axemen worked to clear roads and build bridges
over streams and flooded swamps, while the sound of rebel axemen could be
heard in the distance, felling trees and creating more havoc in the woods.
The marshes were mosquito-ridden, fraught with surprise attacks and snip-

ing. Hours passed slowly for Burgoyne's infantrymen, who had to build fortified camps and stand guard over axemen in the gloomy swamps. When the road was ready, the soldiers would break camp and march a couple of miles, then camp again and fortify for a few more days before breaking camp once more to move a little further on.

For the troops, one of the uplifting sights on that sluggish trek was the appearance of their commander, riding in on a fine charger to encourage and praise them. Few officers of his stature would have deigned to mingle with the rank and file as he did, and they loved him for it. When still a young officer, Burgoyne had written a high-minded code of instructions on the handling of men, based on progressive notions of military discipline and training. An officer, he advised, should not swear at the troops, but rather jest with them as "an encouragement to the well-disposed and at the same time a tacit reproof to others." The officer also should refrain from routine brutal punishment, and he was encouraged to consider the soldier to be a thinking creature, not a puppet.

During that methodical slog through the dank forest toward the Hudson, Burgoyne made his headquarters in a tent near burned-out Fort Anne. Here, he continued his opulent banquets (usually under a shady tree, and as ever with crystal and silver), but in the lonely hours he sent out disguised couriers, who faced certain death as spies if captured.

Burgoyne had to get a report to General Howe in New York, and he was anxious to hear of that officer's plans for movement up the Hudson. He also wanted to know about the force under Colonel Barry St. Leger, which was advancing along the Mohawk, making for Albany. Couriers came to him in the dark of night, so that they would not be recognized by spies in the British camp. Messages written in cipher were hidden in the heels of their boots; others were included in innocuous letters, which, if held against a special stencil, would be revealed. One message was written on fine silk that was wadded into a hollow bullet made of silver, the halves of which unscrewed to come apart.

Few couriers from Burgoyne to headquarters in New York survived their attempts to get through rebel-held country; one who did carried a letter within a letter, which could be read only when a specially made template was laid over it, revealing the secret message.

The volunteers who carried these dispatches had to make their way through enemy pickets facing the royal army, then escape detection by patrols and get past suspicious militia watchmen on guard at every village, every crossroads, everywhere a stranger could be challenged and searched. Then, approaching the British lines at New York, the courier had to slip past more patrols and front-line pickets and avoid being shot by the nervous

British sentry who would demand a password the courier could not know. The man who got through to Howe with a message from Burgoyne was expected to turn around and take the reply back again, retracing his steps from New York. If caught, the courier would die on the spot, hanged from the nearest tree or shot. So far, all the couriers sent southward by Burgoyne— at least half a dozen—had not been heard from. Daily, he looked for a dispatch from Howe.

Burgoyne was increasingly troubled by the lack of information from the Indians, but the loyalist scouts and picked light infantrymen were ranging effectively in front of the army and reporting on enemy movements. On July 11, he wrote Lord Germain a dispatch that was sent along the lengthening line of communication to Montreal, and eventually to London. He told Germain that most of the Indians were still plundering abandoned farms back in the vicinity of Ticonderoga, their behavior increasingly capricious, like "spoiled children." He was trying to control them, but "were they left to themselves, enormities too horrid to think of would ensue; guilty and innocent, women and infants, would be common prey."

The English gentleman-soldier was learning the hard truth of American colonial warfare, and now that the pageantry of the naval advance up Champlain was over, he did not like all he had seen. Further, he had second thoughts about the campaign's objectives in the Hudson Valley. He wrote to London that his orders from Germain gave him too little "latitude" and did not permit him to take the initiative and move against New England. ". . . Were I at liberty to march in force immediately by my left, instead of to my right, I should have little doubt of subduing before winter the province where the rebellion originated."

Meaning Massachusetts. Burgoyne obviously still had a low opinion of the rebel fighting man and expected little resistance.

The expedition was not as strong as it had been, for it had suffered about two hundred casualties, and another thousand troops were left in garrisons strung out along the Champlain Valley, guarding the supply depots, carts, and bateaux. Guards also were needed for the sick and wounded, and for the clutter of camp followers, who included merchants selling food and wares to the troops. Burgoyne asked Governor Carleton to send the troops needed to garrison Ticonderoga, because detaching so many of his own men to defend the line of communications had left the army in a condition that he described as "a little difficult." Carleton, however, did not have enough troops to occupy those lonely outposts from Skenesboro to St.-Jean.

July wore on, with its overpowering humidity and heat, and Burgoyne's army suffered as it kept advancing slowly through forest and swamp. The general had never imagined it would take so long to open the road, but Schuyler's men had been devilishly thorough in their labors to make the woods impassable, criss-crossing and entangling the branches of fallen trees to make clearing the way all the more frustrating.

The mouth of Fort Edward Creek on the Hudson River, where the final phase of the campaign began.

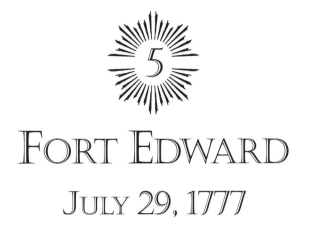

FORT EDWARD

JULY 29, 1777

On this day, Burgoyne's vanguard finally broke out of the suffocating forest and stood on the rolling meadows near Fort Edward, another post abandoned by the rebels at the very last moment. It had taken twenty-three days to come as many miles.

The British not only had lost those days, but had given them to General Schuyler, who was being reinforced daily by Continental troops coming up from Washington's army in the Jerseys and from Pennsylvania and Virginia. Five miles to the south on Moses Creek, and just out of reach of the invading army's new encampment at Fort Edward, Schuyler commanded a strong body of troops. Burgoyne was impatient to get at Schuyler and then start the final push to Albany. For the first time since embarking at St.-Jean, he had the army camped close together, along the road between Fort Edward and the river called the Battenkill. His headquarters marquee was still at Fort Anne, busy with the coming and going of staff officers coordinating the enormous task of transporting supplies.

Burgoyne made frequent rounds of the tent lines and bivouacs. His standing orders forbade observance of the usual formalities due a commander entering the lines, so work or meals were to continue. Whenever the troops were paraded for his review, he saw their spirits were good, uniforms clean and mended. Regimental laundresses, hired from among the camp followers, did their best to issue fresh white linens each Wednesday and Sunday. The soldiers' white or buff-colored waistcoats and breeches were kept as clean as possible, as were the uniform coats, which in the case of the British had been shorn of their long tails last winter.

Those tails had been put to use as patching material, for the uniform coats had not been replaced for far too long. It was the same with the men's well-worn black cocked hats, which also had been trimmed and tailored, changed to a round skullcap. These did not lose their dash, however, for they were in the style of light infantry leather helmets, and had feathers or horse-hair tassels adorning them. Each regiment was identified by the color of its coat's facings (the lapels and turned-back cuffs), with those of the honored "royal" regiments, such as the 21st Foot, a distinctive dark blue. The facings of the 47th were off-white, and other regiments had facings of yellow, white, red, or green. The loyalist rangers wore dark green coats, some with black collar, cuffs, and buttons for camouflage, others with red or blue and buff.

The Germans had their own tradition of uniform design, the dragoons wearing light-blue coats with yellow facings, the infantry in dark-blue coats usually with red, yellow, or white facings. Often, the troops wore canvas overalls to protect their uniforms on the march and on fatigue parties.

The expedition was fit and ready, but Burgoyne wished the loyalist sympathizers were more numerous. It was good to hear that the short-term militias were steadily melting away from the rebel army. Burgoyne also learned that General Horatio Gates, another former British officer, had replaced Schuyler as the American commander. In fact, more than thirty years ago, both Gates and Burgoyne had been young lieutenants in the 20th Regiment of Foot. That mattered little to Burgoyne, however, for he had only contempt for provincial generals.

Ugly tales now came in, of Burgoyne's Indians attacking both rebel and loyalist farmers, shooting horses for the thrill of it, killing cattle just to get the cowbells, which the warriors wanted to hang around their own necks. War parties returned to the army's encampments triumphantly waving fresh scalps stretched on stick frameworks. Few whites with the army could admire that work, though the warriors boasted of killing and scalping only men under arms.

There were more and more reports of settlers being attacked, whole families murdered by the Indians, but Burgoyne did not want to believe them. Then he heard terrible news. The Indians had brought in a Scotswoman, a distant cousin of General Fraser's, who had emigrated years ago to nearby Argyle. Now she raved that her captors had cold-bloodedly murdered and scalped a young woman named Jane McCrea. Jane had been on the way to Burgoyne's army, intending to join her fiance, Lieutenant David Jones, a local man who had enlisted in the loyalist corps. The Scotswoman accused a halfbreed French Iroquois named Le Loup of murdering the girl, just a few miles from the British camp near Fort Edward. Even now, Le Loup strutted around with Jane's scalp, its long tresses hanging from his belt. The general was enraged, for his honor, the honor of the expedition and of the British army, had been stained.

Braunschw. Reg. v. Riedesel
1778.
in America

E. Sack

Brunswickers like this infantryman of the Riedesel Regiment made up most of the German units in Burgoyne's army.

Rebels accused Burgoyne's Indians of cold-bloodedly murdering
Jane McCrea, a local settler and fiancee of a loyalist officer with the
army; the Indians denied it and claimed a rebel scouting party they
encountered accidentally shot her while she was being led away on
horseback toward Burgoyne's lines.

The soldiers were upset when they heard about it, their morale badly
shaken. Disgrace threatened the high-mindedness of Burgoyne's cause.
Something had to be done. He demanded that Le Loup be court-martialed
and, if found guilty, executed as an example to prove how opposed the
general was to wanton killing. It would not, however, be so simple.

Burgoyne's closest counselors, including Fraser, cautioned him not to
take hasty action against Le Loup, a respected translator who had much in-
fluence over the warriors. If Le Loup were punished, the Indians not only
would abandon the army, but would lurk on its fringes, killing and robbing
Burgoyne's men if they had the chance. They might even go over to the
rebels. One of the French-Canadian leaders warned that if Burgoyne

hanged Le Loup, there would be massacres of unprotected Canadian villages as bands of angry warriors made their way homeward.

Le Loup denied the accusation of Burgoyne's board of inquiry, which found that he had killed the young woman during an argument with another warrior who had wanted to bring her in as his own prisoner. In fact, Le Loup declared, Jane had been accidentally shot in a clash between his war party and a rebel patrol. Naturally, he had taken the scalp from the dead woman.

Burgoyne forced himself, "for the good of the service," to issue Le Loup a pardon. Then he ordered the Indians to come in for another conference. None of this did the army's spirits any good, for the men were ashamed of the raids by the Indians. An English officer wrote home that "the cruelties committed by them were too shocking to relate."

Before the Indian council took place, Burgoyne heard that three of four couriers recently sent to Howe in New York had been caught, two of them executed, the fate of the third unknown. So far, after almost eight weeks in the field, he had no idea what Howe was doing, nor had there been much communication with St. Leger somewhere on the Mohawk River.

Burgoyne moved his headquarters to Fort Edward, in the large red house of Patrick Smythe, a loyalist who had fled to Canada. On August 3, the long-anticipated fourth courier returned with a letter from Howe, but the message was dismaying. Howe warmly congratulated Burgoyne on his success at Ticonderoga, then added almost casually that his own army was about to go southward by sea to attack the rebel capital at Philadelphia, "where I expect to meet Washington, but if he goes to the northward . . . and you can keep him at bay, be assured I shall soon be after him to relieve you. After your arrival in Albany, the movements of the enemy will guide yours."

There was no mention of any direct orders from Germain instructing Howe to move on Albany, a plan approved by King George himself! Why not? Howe seemed to think Burgoyne's campaign was as good as won and there was no need to send an army up the Hudson River. Howe said General Sir Henry Clinton would be left in command of New York, and if the situation warranted it, might be able to make a diversionary attack up the river to lend Burgoyne a hand. Now it appeared that no more than a minor move could be hoped from New York unless Germain's orders arrived in time to change Howe's plans.

It was deeply troubling to Burgoyne, although he held out the hope that another dispatch soon would get through to him announcing that Howe finally had received Lord Germain's direct orders to move north. In the grip of doubt, Burgoyne decided to keep Howe's troubling letter a secret for now, even from his closest officers.

Some in Burgoyne's staff already had suggested leaving all extra baggage behind, even the artillery train, and rushing down the west side of the Hudson to attack the enemy's main position near Stillwater. The general did not want to move so recklessly, though, for there was the problem of sufficient provisions, and he was determined to have enough artillery on hand. After Breed's Hill, he would permit no frontal assaults until the enemy was driven from its defenses by cannon fire.

The general still hoped to coordinate his advance with the garrison in New York, but there was more troubling news that St. Leger was delayed by resistance in the Mohawk Valley. In the meantime, he had to hold the council with the Indians.

Burgoyne had plenty to trouble him on August 4, when he went to the Indian encampment near Fort Edward. Unlike that first heady war council at the Boquet River, this was not an excited gathering of a warlike host setting out on the road of certain triumph. The warriors resented Burgoyne's anger with them, and they sat sullen and arrogant, many sporting the fresh scalps and booty they had taken.

Frustrated that the campaign was not going according to plan, Burgoyne did his best to put on a dignified face, and he made yet another flowery speech to the Indians, reasserting his demand that they not attack noncombatants. In reply, they again solemnly promised to obey the rules of civilized warfare. By next morning, most of the Indians and French-Canadian scouts had deserted the army. The cloud of warriors meant to blind the rebels had abandoned Burgoyne.

With the murder of Jane McCrea, irreversible damage had been done. Not only were the loyalists disappointed in him—the sorrowful Lieutenant Jones bought Jane's scalp, resigned, and went back to Canada—but Burgoyne's use of Indians had the opposite effect on the provincial militia he intended to frighten. Schuyler sent riders far and wide, announcing the killing of Jane, calling on militias to speed their march against "hair-buyer" Burgoyne. Most New York and New England militias already had been ordered out, but until now Burgoyne had been aware of only tentative gatherings in the Hampshire Grants to the east. Lately, reports were coming in that thousands of militia were marching against him there.

Brigadier General Simon Fraser, a Scotsman, was an experienced campaigner in North America and had relatives living in the upper Hudson Valley.

He soon informed Germain that the forces in the eastern mountains were "the most rebellious race in the continent," hanging "like a gathering storm on my left." Where were the hordes of loyalist sympathizers that had been expected to rise and fight with him to preserve the British empire against a tyrannical Congress?

There followed an exchange of harsh letters between Burgoyne and the new rebel commander, Horatio Gates, debating the facts and circumstances of the Jane McCrea affair. That the "famous" Burgoyne, "in whom the fine gentleman is united with the soldier and the scholar, should hire the savages of America to scalp Europeans and the descendants of Europeans," wrote Gates, "nay more, that he should pay a price for each scalp so barbarously taken, is more than will be believed in England until authenticated facts shall in every gazette convince mankind of the truth of this horrid tale."

In reply, Burgoyne "lamented" the McCrea killing, characterizing it as "no premeditated barbarity" but the result of a dispute between two jealous captors. He denied that Indian atrocities were widespread, saying, "I condescend to inform you that I would not be conscious of the acts you presume to impute to me for the whole continent of

A Brunswick infantryman of the Specht Regiment.

America, though the wealth of worlds were in its bowels and a paradise on its surface." He insisted that pardoning the killer was the most sensible and safest course to follow.

No matter what Burgoyne said, Gates had the upper hand, and Burgoyne was on the defensive in more ways than one: his Indians were mostly gone; loyalist volunteers were too few; apparently Howe was not coming, and perhaps neither was Clinton; St. Leger had been held up trying to besiege Fort Stanwix on the Mohawk; and the long supply line to Canada could not be protected against rebel raids. Once Burgoyne launched his final advance on Albany, there was no margin for error, because an orderly retreat northward would be extremely difficult, if not impossible. Even in the event of a successful retreat, however, it was certain that his star would no longer be on the rise. His enemies in Parliament would attack him for enlisting Indians and for the death of Jane McCrea, not to mention the mockery they would make of his widely known boast that he would return home victorious by Christmas Day.

A man with Burgoyne's spirit, ambition, and gambler's instinct could only plunge ahead. He must lead his army across the Hudson, force the rebels into the open, and smash them decisively.

The Hudson River fording place at Fort Miller was often used
by war parties, militia, and regular forces during the colonial
wars in America.

FORT MILLER

AUGUST 11, 1777

After two weeks in the red house near Fort Edward, with the main British army camped just south of the old earth-and-log fort, Burgoyne moved his quarters farther down the river to Fort Miller.

Named for French and Indian War defensive works that once had stood across the river, this little community was near a strategic ford that in years past had been used by many a fighting force. All that was left of the old fort was the foundation of a blockhouse that had guarded the ford, which was just below swift rapids. At Fort Miller, Burgoyne took up residence in a fine brick house owned by William Duer, a Scotsman who once had served on the staff of Lord Clive in India, and who was a delegate to the Continental Congress.

Plans were made for the army to cross the Hudson near here, and then begin its march down the west shore to Albany. More than ever, with a decisive battle not far off, the German dragoons must have horses. The farms in the hills to the east had plenty of horses, and the rebels were building a supply depot at the village of Bennington, twenty-eight miles away. Burgoyne decided to send the Germans on a raid in strength to capture the rebel magazine, said to be guarded by only four hundred militiamen. If successful, the expedition might even keep on marching eastward before turning south to rejoin the main army.

In command of the force was Lieutenant Colonel Friedrich Baum, who would lead seven hundred men, two-thirds of them Germans. With

Baum would go the Queen's Loyal Rangers under John Peters, and some of the remaining *Canadiens* and Indians would be the scouts. One crucial object was to raise the nearby loyalists, who, Philip Skene insisted, were waiting to be "liberated" from the rebel yoke. Skene would go along as liaison with the provincials. He said they were in favor of the king by at least five to one, but Burgoyne warned that no one was to be trusted as loyal until it was clear they were not spies or subversives.

Skene insisted the rebels would never stand and fight in a large body, and said the campaign could only be won by the operations of strong detachments such as Baum's. Adamant about the shortcomings of the rebels, Skene said, "The Americans want confidence in their officers and their officers want confidence in them."

Braunschw: Dragoner Regt.
1778
Kail
J. v Germann

Braunschw: Jäger,
1778.
Kail
J. v Germann

Burgoyne said Baum would encounter some rebel troops, even Continentals, but they would retreat in the face of so strong a force. Baron Riedesel objected to that assumption, but he was overruled by both Burgoyne and General Phillips. Then General Fraser said John Peters believed Skene was wrong, that the local people were not loyal, and that the country was extremely dangerous for Baum. After years of living here, Peters knew the region well and believed at least three thousand men were required to accomplish this mission.

Hearing such a blunt contradiction, Burgoyne exploded in anger, telling Fraser, "When I want your advice, I shall ask for it!" He then declared all Americans to be no more than disobedient cowards.

(Opposite, left) Brunswick dragoons, wearing infantry gear because the regiment had not brought horses to America. They were expected to fight as infantry in most of this campaign.

(Opposite, right) A Brunswick *Jaeger*, or "hunter," was a sharpshooter who served as a scout and skirmisher, prepared for operating in the wilderness of the Champlain Valley.

(Right) A Brunswick infantryman of the Prince Friedrich Regiment.

Braunschw. Regt Prinz Friedrich
1778.
F. v Germann
kail

In response, Peters calmly spoke up, saying "I am ready to obey your orders, General Burgoyne, but we shall not return."

At dawn on August 13, Burgoyne mounted his charger and, with aide Sir Francis Clarke riding at his side, cantered out to review Baum's departing force. The general took the salute of the heavily laden Brunswick infantry marching in ranks four abreast and singing Lutheran hymns. Also in the force were a hundred big grenadiers, a few green-jacketed *Jaegers*, and a hundred and fifty Brunswick dragoons with their three-foot sabers.

Behind the column rumbled two field guns, then came the supply train and the straggling mob of German camp followers. There was no telling how long this expedition would last, but if it went well the ultimate goal was Brattleboro, on the Connecticut River seventy miles to the east.

As the German column entered the forest on the narrow, rutted track, Burgoyne and his aide trotted away toward the Duer house to oversee preparations for the march against Gates. Less than twenty miles away, near Stillwater, the rebels were building earthworks to block the only road along the Hudson. The British would outflank those works and get between them and Albany, drawing the rebels out for an honorable fight that trained troops undoubtedly would win.

Fraser and his advance brigade crossed the Hudson on the floating bridge of rafts.

Early the next morning, Burgoyne was awakened at the Duer house by the arrival of a courier from Baum, and the news was troubling. The rebels near Bennington numbered far more than four hundred: at least eighteen hundred were mustered there, commanded by John Stark, the war-wise former Rogers Ranger, who was a respected hero of the French and Indian War and one of the rebel commanders at Bunker Hill.

Before Burgoyne could respond to this unexpected development, another courier came galloping in from Baum, this time with a request for immediate reinforcements. Acting quickly, Burgoyne ordered out the German troops commanded by Lieutenant Colonel Heinrich Breymann, urging them to move as fast as possible to support Baum.

The second column, with two more cannon, was on the rutted road by nine o'clock that morning, but these troops would not be the quickest reinforcement. Most were grenadiers in tall, silver-mitered caps, and their officers were accustomed to halting them again and again to form up in ranks and march in parade-ground order, no matter how bad the roads.

Burgoyne had much to do all that day and the next, his troops and workmen laboring hard, sweltering in the heat as they loaded guns, supplies, and equipment into the bateaux. Ten tons of provisions were consumed every day, all brought from Canada, first by water over Lake Champlain, then unloaded to be portaged by cart to Lake George, reloaded into bateaux, and shipped to a supply depot at the head of the lake. From there it all was put back in carts and slowly hauled to the army on the Hudson. (By now, Fort George had been abandoned by the rebels without a fight.) The general lamented that he worked one hour at strategy for every twenty hours organizing means of provision. Despite all this distraction, he was increasingly anxious to hear about Baum.

Then it began to rain, a dismal summer downpour that lasted all day and into the night. The river rose to a torrent, and by morning the bridge linking the army to Fraser's advance corps on the west bank had been swept away. Burgoyne ordered every available craft to ferry Fraser's unsupported troops back to the east shore until the bridge could be rebuilt. The rain stopped by the evening of August 16, and Burgoyne went to bed still not knowing what had happened on the road to Bennington. Again he was awakened early, this time by a haggard French-Canadian officer who had been with Baum. The news was disastrous: Baum had been killed, most of his seven hundred men dead or prisoners.

The slow-moving Breymann had arrived too late to be of help, but he also had suffered heavy casualties when the rebels attacked him in turn. All four guns had been lost. The Indians had slipped away into the woods when the fighting became most desperate, abandoning the Germans and loyalists to their fates. Even worse, before the Indians departed the area, they ambushed, murdered, and robbed some of the soldiers who had been their allies. Now, the woods were full of wandering Germans and loyalists trying to find their way back to the army.

Burgoyne hurriedly ordered out the 47th Foot and took personal command of the rescue force. He rode at the head of the column, double-timing along the forest road, but they had not gone far when Breymann appeared on horseback, leading his column of utterly exhausted men. Seeing Burgoyne, the Germans straightened up and dressed their lines, though many were wounded, all of them battle-weary. The somber Burgoyne and Breymann drew up their horses, facing each other a moment, and the German removed his hat to bow. Agony from a leg wound jarred through him, and he flushed from the pain. His coat was torn with bullet holes from near-misses.

Composing himself, Burgoyne bowed low and gave a brief speech, thanking Breymann and the troops "for their very pretty little success" and saying the enemy would feel their own losses from the battle "most severely." Turning to the commander of the 47th, Burgoyne ordered the English regiment to line the road as a guard of honor for the beaten Germans. With Burgoyne and Breymann riding side by side, the grenadiers summoned their pride and began to sing as they marched, many limping, through the avenue of dismayed and wondering Redcoats.

By now, Burgoyne had not only lost a quarter of his German troops and most of his Indians, but it was clear there would be no major rallying of armed loyalists. Peters Corps alone had lost more than a hundred men, fighting courageously in the Bennington defeat. Peters himself was wounded but managed to rejoin the army.

Burgoyne learned that a large number of provincials had pretended to be loyalists and joined Baum's Germans on the march to Bennington. Then, at a signal, the provincials had opened fire, point-blank, killing and wounding many in the very first moments of the fight. Despite the great heart of the Germans, they had been doomed almost before the battle started.

Once again Burgoyne had not been obeyed, for he had warned Skene, who also had escaped, against trusting professed loyalists. At his field desk in the Duer house, Burgoyne composed a grim dispatch to Lord Germain.

"When I wrote more confidently, I little foresaw that I was to be left to pursue my way through such a tract of country and hosts of foes, without any cooperation from New York. . . . The great bulk of the country is undoubtedly with the Congress, in principle and in zeal; and their measures are executed with a secrecy and dispatch that are not to be equaled. Wherever the King's forces point, militia assemble in twenty-four hours."

He said General Gates was in a strong position and had "an army superior to mine in troops of the Congress and as many militia as he pleases. He is likewise far from being deficient in artillery. . . ." Then Burgoyne explained why he would continue southward despite his worsening condition. ". . . I should think it my duty to wait in this position, or perhaps as far back as Fort Edward, where my communication with Lake George would be perfectly secure, till some event happened to assist my movement forward; but my orders being positive to 'force a junction with Sir William Howe,' I apprehend that I am not at liberty to remain inactive longer [than required to build up enough supplies]."

Burgoyne said he would obey his orders as he understood them, but he must make his move soon so that if he met "insurmountable difficulties" there would still be "the chance of fighting my way back to Ticonderoga." If he waited too long without attacking or retreating, the weather would turn cold, and "a retreat might be shut in by impenetrable bars of the elements, and at the same time no possible means of existence remain in the country."

Once he got through to Albany, he would fortify there and await Howe's support. "Whatever should be my fate . . . whatever decision may be passed

The royal army advanced down the east bank of the Hudson River
while heavy equipment and supplies were carried by bateaux that
had been carted overland from the lakes.

upon my conduct, my good intent will not be questioned." As ever throughout his career, Burgoyne did not fail to praise his officers and men, "expressing my fullest satisfaction in the behaviour and countenance of the troops."

By early September, reports came in that the rebels had captured a provision vessel and gunboats on Lake George. The small garrisons were at risk, with Ticonderoga being the object of enemy troops massing north and east of Burgoyne's army. Then, one of the few couriers to get through arrived from Barry St. Leger. Another blow struck. St. Leger had been stopped by militia and Continentals on the Mohawk, forced to retreat all the way back to Lake Ontario.

By now, Burgoyne had changed his opinion of the provincial fighting man. After St. Leger's repulse and the cool battlefield conduct of rebel militia under John Stark and Continentals under Seth Warner near Bennington, the general had developed a grudging respect. He had hinted as much in his dispatch to Germain when he pointedly mentioned the presence of Continentals, the "troops of the Congress," with Gates.

More than ever, Burgoyne found himself facing a moment of truth: advance against a growing enemy army or withdraw to Canada, humiliated, and with heavy losses. This was the time to inform the army that Howe was in Pennsylvania and would not be marching to join them. When Burgoyne did so, the men were astonished and confused, for they had expected to be supported; but they did not show fear. Tough, hardened, they would go anywhere the general led them.

Burgoyne made the decision that most of his officers and men wholeheartedly endorsed: the army would cross the Hudson on the pontoon bridge and advance toward Albany. This was as bold a move as any they could make, but there were no illusions among his rank and file. One officer wrote to an acquaintance in the House of Commons, saying if the general could extricate himself from the difficulties that surrounded him, "future ages would have little occasion to talk of Hannibal and his escape."

The most seriously wounded were sent back to Canada, and unnecessary baggage and excess clothing were shipped to Ticonderoga so the troops would be as unencumbered as possible. No more supplies were to be forwarded from Ticonderoga. The army faced southward.

On the chilly afternoon of September 11, Burgoyne's force prepared to move out, but rain suddenly poured down so heavily that he canceled his orders. The troops once more pitched their tents, and the pontoon bridge had to be taken apart again to prevent rising water from washing it away. Cold rain soaked everyone and everything, a foretaste of the autumn that was not far off. Wet wood did not burn, it was difficult to start fires, and the shivering men in their summer uniforms began to wish they had not sent their warm underclothes and coats back to Fort Ti.

The morning of September 13 was sunny and dry as the troops paraded, ready to move out. The bridge was reassembled, and by early afternoon Burgoyne's vanguard hurried across. As the main army filed over the Hudson, they saw their commander on horseback with his staff, looking down at them from high ground on the opposite bank. The troops cheered as they marched past, and Burgoyne lifted his plumed hat in reply, calling out again and again, "Britons never retreat!"

Hours later, after the army was over the river, along with the supply train, artillery, officers' wives and families in their calashes, the camp followers, and finally the 47th Foot rear guard, Burgoyne ordered the bridge dismantled. It would be floated downriver along with the supply bateaux, keeping up as the army advanced. Until those pontoons were rejoined, there was no way Burgoyne could recross the Hudson, not even if he had to.

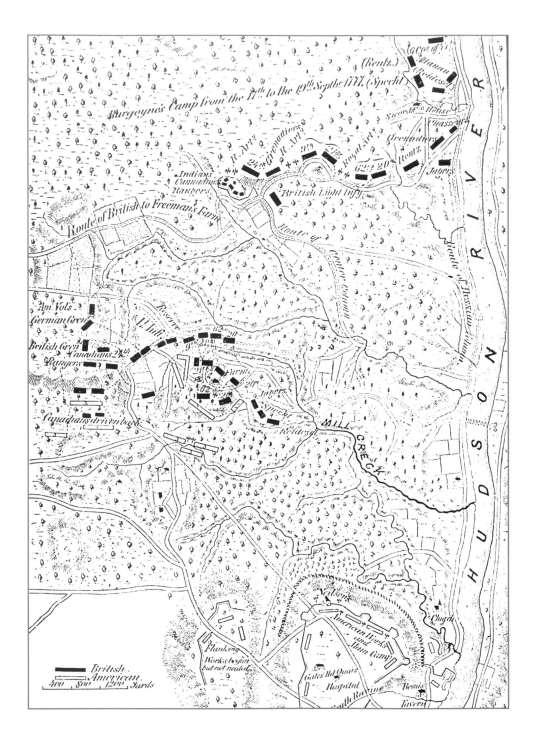

The first battle of Saratoga has been called the Battle of Sword's House, the First Battle of Freeman's Farm, Bemis Heights, and Stillwater.

FREEMAN'S FARM

SEPTEMBER 17, 1777

Burgoyne's grim army advanced toward Albany on the narrow road along the west shore of the Hudson. It crossed over a creek called the Fishkill near General Schuyler's fine country home, and passed through the hamlet of Saratoga.

The ground on the army's right rose steeply, most of it woods, but the road ran through low-lying farm fields that had been harvested or burned by the retreating rebels to prevent the invaders from gathering in the crops. Yesterday, a spontaneous foraging party of thirty men and a few women had found a patch of potatoes and went to dig them up. They were ambushed there, some killed, many captured. The general was furious to "lose men for the pitiful consideration of potatoes," and he issued a standing order that no soldiers were to go beyond the advanced sentries, or they would be arrested and "instantly hanged."

That very night, a fire in young Major John Acland's tent almost cost his life and that of his pregnant wife, Harriet. Acland, the popular commander of the grenadiers, had been painfully burned, and the near-fatal mishap had not helped the mood of the jittery troops.

As for the Germans, far too many of their comrades had fallen because of what they considered Burgoyne's mistakes. Their officers, especially Riedesel, had lost confidence in the general, but the troops were dependable—though a few were slipping away as deserters. A core of staunch loyalist rangers was still with the army, but only a few Indians and French-Canadians remained for the coming battle.

By now, the rebels owned the countryside all around, and even the best scouts were in danger of being ambushed. Burgoyne was operating almost blindly. His rear-echelon units such as hospitals, magazines, artillery park, and transport had to be kept close to the main body, and were set up near the river at a gully called the Great Ravine. He made his headquarters a few miles past Saratoga in a farmhouse of a family named Sword. The house and barns stood at the fork of a creek about five hundred yards from the river, with a long view down a row of trees leading to the Hudson.

The general and his staff made final the plan for attacking Gates, who was strongly fortified six miles away on Bemis Heights near Stillwater. Three German regiments under Baron Riedesel would advance along the road, as if to attack the enemy earthworks. Meanwhile, General Fraser would lead his corps around to the right on a narrow track through the woods to the farm of John Freeman, a loyalist who had fled to Canada. The general meant to choose the place of battle, to meet the rebels in the Freeman fields, which would favor his army's close-order tactics.

Fraser also would maneuver toward the Freeman farmhouse and there rejoin Burgoyne, who would lead four regiments in the center, with Riedesel on the left. All three corps would operate separately until Burgoyne decided they were abreast of one another. Then he would have a cannon fire three times to order the general advance of the army and an artillery barrage against the rebel fortifications. Burgoyne and Fraser would attack the left of Gates's army, bringing their full weight upon that flank.

On the night of September 18, the entire army looked to its equipment and prepared to attack. Burgoyne spent hours with young officers, playing cards and drinking wine before returning briefly at dawn to the company of his mistress.

The morning hung with dense mist, delaying the three corps from leaving their bivouacs. When they finally moved out, Burgoyne was at the head of his troops, with a thin line of skirmishers thrown in front. His road followed the twisting course of a stream flowing through terrain that was unexpectedly rough, overgrown and broken up with ravines.

The regiments under his command were among the best in the British Army, and the artillery also was first-rate, but neither gunners nor infantry had gone into battle in such densely overgrown country before. They struggled through entangling thickets and over washed-out trails, and it was not until early afternoon that they finally reached the jumping off point at the

British artillery crews were cut down by rebel rifle fire as they tried to man their guns.

north end of Freeman's farm. The sunlit fields sloping to the south were a welcome relief from the woods, but the far treeline a couple of hundred yards off was dark and silent. There, the rebels might be waiting.

On command, the British skirmishers advanced into the open, and now they saw men at the far treeline. Suddenly rifles fired, gun smoke puffing from the opposite woods, even from up in treetops. Virtually all the British officers in the front ranks fell, dead or wounded. The Redcoat skirmishers fell back toward Burgoyne's main force, and across the field appeared rebels in fringed shirts, aiming and firing as they moved forward. The Americans came too far. With a mighty shout Burgoyne's men fired a volley and charged, driving them back into the woods. The rifle fire slowed, and the distant squawk of a turkey call could be heard, obviously a signal to the rebels. Ordering a cannon fired three times at one-minute intervals, Burgoyne commanded Fraser and Riedesel to advance.

There was more movement in the far woods, as of fresh troops joining the enemy riflemen. Burgoyne's ranks opened a steady volley fire at them, a tremendous roar that, with the blasts of cannon, almost deafened the soldiers. The rebels did not withdraw, however. No distinct enemy line could be seen, but their fire was more deadly than ever, and the exposed Redcoats began to fall. Bullets whizzed around the general, a sound like swarms of bees, but he rode calmly back and forth along the line, encouraging the men, urging on his officers, all the while heedless of the lead that tore at his coat. Officers of all units were targets, Burgoyne, on his charger, the most exposed of all. When a bullet clipped his plumed hat, he only laughed, holding the hat aloft for his men to see. The troops laughed with him and cheered his courage.

The infantry suffered severely as they stood and fired. The 62nd Foot paid especially dearly, standing in the open and exchanging fire with unseen enemies. Artillerymen, too, were cut down, picked off one after the other as they served their guns. Entire crews of twenty men were wiped out. At last, the British had to withdraw from the fields to the cover of a stand of pines. The rebels were so elated at driving regulars from the field that they again began to attack, leaving their cover and advancing. Once more the situation was reversed, with the rebels exposed, and they lost heavily until, through the roar of gunfire, a turkey call again rang out, and they withdrew.

The call that pierced the din of battle seemed to hang over the fields after the enemy fell back to the cover of the woods, and the firing slowed.

It was an eerie sound.

Then rebel gunfire began working its way around the British left. They were trying to outflank Burgoyne. Firing became hotter as more rebels arrived, moving farther around his flank. He needed support from Fraser or Riedesel. Where were they? When Fraser's aide rode up, it was to tell the general that Fraser was holding on the right and could not join him in force or send substantial reinforcements. As the general and aide talked, sitting close together on their horses, the aide suddenly lurched from the saddle, wounded by a marksman, who might just as well have targeted Burgoyne.

The situation became steadily worse until, just when Burgoyne felt he was outflanked, almost cut off, a mass of Germans in blue coats

62ᵈ Regiment
1778.

F. v. German

The British 62nd Regiment was almost wiped out in the first battle of Saratoga.

charged out of the trees on his left, their cannon blasting the rebels. The enemy vanished from the far treeline and the firing slowed as the Brunswickers swept through the woods. Burgoyne had been rescued by Riedesel.

When darkness came on, the exhausted Redcoats had held the ground, but at an awful cost they could not afford. Almost seven hundred had been

Under constant rebel cannonading, Baroness von Riedesel took shelter in this farmhouse, along with women, children, and wounded soldiers.

killed or wounded, most of them British, including several of Burgoyne's key officers. The 62nd had lost the heaviest, with only sixty men fit for duty from more than two hundred and eighty who had set out that morning. The men buried as many of the dead of both armies as possible, and in one grave lay three ensigns of the 20th Foot, the oldest only seventeen.

Hurrying back to his headquarters tent set up at the Great Ravine, Burgoyne had to rethink his strategy. There waited the anxious wives of officers, one of whom learned her husband was wounded, and another that hers was dead. Nearby, the field hospital filled up with groaning, screaming wounded, who were cared for by a few overwhelmed surgeons and the wives of the soldiers.

Though immensely weary, Burgoyne told his commanders to prepare to resume the attack at first light. In his dispatches that night, with the sound of agony all around, he claimed victory, for he had held the field. In truth, he had been stopped.

One soldier could have been speaking for his general when he wrote home: "The courage and obstinacy with which the Americans fought were the astonishment of everyone, and we now become fully convinced they are not that contemptible enemy we had hitherto imagined them, incapable of standing a regular engagement, and that they would only fight behind strong and powerful works."

Rebel artillery fire drove Baroness von Riedesel and other noncombatants into this cellar to escape cannonballs that crashed into the house.

The turkey call had been the signal of Colonel Daniel Morgan, commander of the Virginia rifleman who had been sent north by Washington. Morgan was yet another seasoned veteran of the French and Indian War. The rebels had many experienced leaders, perhaps even more than did the royal army.

After lying on their firearms all night in bone-chilling cold, the exhausted troops doggedly formed up at dawn. Again, heavy fog cloaked everything, and the weary men waited hour after hour for it to rise. At last, General Fraser opposed the attack, saying the men had to rest. Burgoyne accepted this—the soldiers loved Fraser even more than him—and called on his staff to formulate plans for another assault within two days. To Burgoyne's amazement, a courier slipped through the lines on September 21 with a letter from Clinton in New York. Clinton would make a thrust up the Hudson toward Albany to capture rebel forts on the highlands. He expected reinforcements soon, but until then this diversion was all he could do for Burgoyne.

For the first time since the Bennington defeat, there was hope, and Burgoyne clung to it. He called off the next assault, choosing to wait until word came of Clinton's advance, which would compel Gates to turn and face the British from that direction as well. As the men dug fortifications, Burgoyne pondered his next move. There were twelve or fourteen thousand rebels before him, with thousands more swarming on his flanks, and his provisions would last only until October 20.

In a dispatch to the commander of Fort Ticonderoga, he wrote: "The difficulties of a retreat to Canada were clearly foreseen, as was the dilemma of leaving at liberty such an army as General Gates's to operate against Sir William Howe." The uniting of Gates with Washington "might possibly decide the fate of the war." If Burgoyne's army had to be "devoted"—sacrificed—to prevent the enemy combining forces, then perhaps that was "only a partial misfortune."

On the nights of September 22 and 23, Burgoyne ordered a cannonade of the enemy positions, and in the tumult sent out two couriers to explain the army's grave situation to Clinton. He wanted to know whether Clinton would move on Albany. If Clinton's reply did not arrive by October 12, Burgoyne would retire northward as best he could.

Though it was of little comfort to him now, a dispatch from England informed him he had been promoted to Lieutenant General.

The royal army waited. The rebels did the same.

October arrived, and with it the realization that Clinton's saving expedition was not at hand. Also with October came the need to reduce daily rations. The weather grew colder and wetter. Conditions in the camp were miserable. Rains uncovered bodies not buried deeply enough. At night, wolves in the woods howled over the unburied dead and pawed up shallow graves. Their wails carried across the muddy redoubts and trenches. The stench of death lingered, from the Brunswick fortifications on the right to the crowded hospital of rough bark huts and tents near the river, where supply bateaux were tied up beside pontoon bridge sections. There were eight hundred sick and wounded, the most serious with little hope of recovery unless they got back to hospitals in Canada. That was probably impossible with so many rebels everywhere.

Uniforms stayed wet for days on end, with no change of clothes. At night, the men were almost frozen, and a soldier wrote that "sleep was a stranger to us." Neither Burgoyne nor his troops were able to take off their uniforms to sleep because the Americans were constantly harassing outposts and firing on the redoubts, as if threatening to attack. The food was

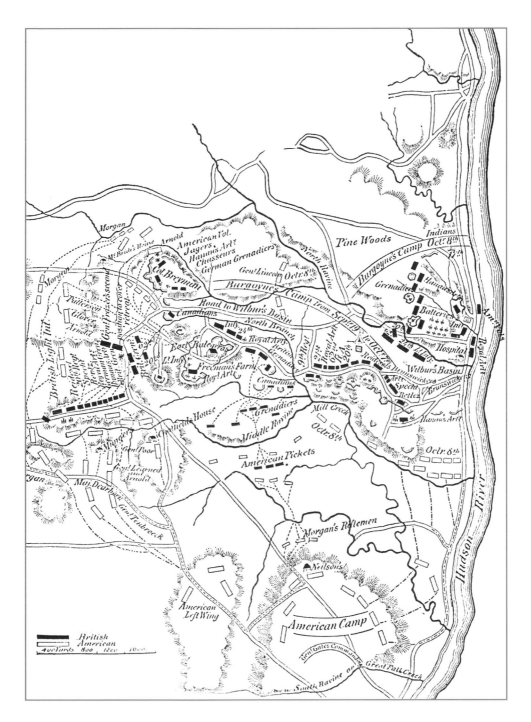

On October 7 the rebels under Gates awaited Burgoyne's attack,
then counterattacked and drove him back to new positions that
soon had to be abandoned.

salt pork and more salt pork, morning and evening. Yet the army was game, morale high. One soldier wrote home that they "were all in good spirits and ready to obey with cheerfulness any orders the General might issue. . . ." He said Burgoyne had "shunned no danger" in battle, and "his presence and conduct animated the troops, for they greatly loved the General."

At last, on Saturday, October 4, Burgoyne held a council of war with Riedesel, Phillips, and Fraser. He told them the bad news that Ticonderoga had been assaulted in a four-day attack by more than fifteen hundred rebel militia. Although the fort had held out, and the rebels withdrew, Burgoyne believed there was no way back now. He wanted to leave only two hundred soldiers to guard the camp, then march the entire force around the American left and attack from the rear.

Riedesel and Fraser disagreed. They recommended immediate retreat to Fort Edward. The river road to there was still under British control, but militia from the Hampshire Grants might appear any day and block it. No final decision was made as yet, but Burgoyne persuaded his commanders to make a reconnaissance in force to test the enemy's strength and willingness to fight. If a full-scale attack was not justified, then Burgoyne would retreat.

At midnight on Sunday, October 5, Burgoyne ordered the firing of a signal rocket, and those who saw it rise and burst wondered whether the general had news that Clinton's force was at hand. There was excitement in the camp, as faces turned southward, watching the sky for some answering rocket to flare. There was none. Burgoyne was only hoping.

On October 6 an extra ration of rum was issued to the troops, who knew that meant they would go into battle the next day.

October 7 broke bright and cloudless as a British and German force of fifteen hundred men formed up in fields on the right, ready to advance.

All four generals—Burgoyne, Phillips, Fraser, and Riedesel—were with the reconnaissance. They stood together on the roof of a log cabin, looking with spyglasses across the fields for some sign of the enemy. If this probing

The site of Freeman's farm is seen in the distant right of this nineteenth-century sketch, which shows the higher ground at center where Fraser's force advanced toward the rebel entrenchments, in the foreground; the second battle took place beyond the woods, in the left distance.

advance discovered weakness in the American defense, then Burgoyne's entire force would follow up the next day with an assault. If the Americans were too strong, the army would withdraw back up the river, as Fraser and Riedesel wanted.

The generals mounted up and rode to their troops. Drums rolled and fifes shrilled. This was no surprise attack. The men stepped out across the fields, forming a line about a thousand yards long, glorious in the October sunlight, flags flying, the undulating waves of bayonets sloped for the advance. They did not get far.

There came the crash of rifles from the forest ahead, followed by a howl as thousands of rebels rushed headlong at the king's troops, who wavered, held their ground, wavered, and rallied. Burgoyne rode back and forth, directing what he could, encouraging by example, always in sight, his hat and waistcoat torn by bullets. He fell once when his horse was shot,

In the second battle of Saratoga, the fatal wounding of General
Simon Fraser, Burgoyne's key subordinate commander, marked the
beginning of the end for the royal army.

but immediately remounted another. The battle raged, and Burgoyne miraculously remained unhurt, but the rebels were too many, too determined. He saw firsthand their willingness to face volley fire and cannonades, even to meet a bayonet charge by grenadiers, blow for blow. At last, he knew he must retreat.

The army gave ground slowly, and Fraser coordinated a skillful withdrawal, ordering counterattacks, concentrating his regiments to prevent a rout. Bullets nicked his horse, and he struggled to keep it from bolting. Someone begged him to take cover, for enemy riflemen were obviously aiming at him. Fraser refused, and in the next instant he was shot in the stomach. He swayed, aides catching him from falling off his horse. The stunned Burgoyne rode alongside as they took Fraser to the house where the officers' ladies were listening to the terrifying roar of gunfire coming ever closer. When Burgoyne departed to direct the withdrawal, he knew his friend's wound was mortal. This was the darkest moment so far.

He sent aide Sir Francis Clarke to order the right wing to withdraw to the redoubts. The rebels followed close behind and turned captured artillery on the royal troops. At last, the survivors of the reconnaissance force reached the shelter of earthworks. The rebels kept after them. Burgoyne took command of the central redoubt and repelled the attack. For the moment, there was a lull in the fighting. As the weary British and Germans waited to see what the enemy would do next, the sun began to go down.

Again the rebels charged at Burgoyne's redoubt, howling and firing, inspired by an officer on a plunging chestnut horse. Burgoyne's troops opened fire, and their cannon mowed the enemy down, but they kept attacking, struggling to get over the pointed branches that blocked the front of the earthworks. The mounted officer galloped back and forth, urging them onward, and with great courage in the face of destructive gunfire they tried to get into the defensive works.

Once more the Americans were repelled, but they stayed en masse in a line of attack, firing steadily at the British and German defenders. From time to time, a group of rebels would shout and rush forward, trying to break through, only to be shot down or driven back. The man on the chestnut horse called over and over for new assaults, heedless of his own life as he led them forward. After yet another repulse, this officer went galloping to Burgoyne's right, across the front of both armies, as everyone held his fire. Burgoyne's men watched him in awe. He was General Benedict Arnold, who had built and led the rebel fleet on Lake Champlain last year, and who had marched a column of Continentals against St. Leger and forced his retreat from the Mohawk Valley. Now Arnold urged on a new attack, this time at the German redoubt on the right, where Breymann commanded a few hundred troops.

The redoubt was out of Burgoyne's sight, but the din of battle from there rose to a furious pitch as the Germans fired volleys. Then the firing abruptly ebbed and stopped. The fighting at Breymann's redoubt was over. Burgoyne could not deny that the redoubt might have fallen.

Darkness came on. Firing slowed everywhere. Burgoyne soon learned Breymann was dead, and his men had all surrendered. With that attack, Arnold had turned Burgoyne's flank. The army had suffered almost nine hundred more casualties in this battle, including two hundred known dead and two hundred and forty prisoners. At one place, fifty grenadiers and three officers lay dead or dying in a space twenty yards square. There was no other choice now but to retreat under cover of darkness, which Burgoyne proceeded to do. He wearily regrouped at positions near the Great Ravine, preparing to withdraw through Saratoga and escape across the Hudson to Fort Edward. If it was not too late.

The house where Fraser died.

First, the dying General Fraser had asked for burial in a redoubt on a hilltop overlooking the river. Before the retreat began, Burgoyne must honor his friend's last request.

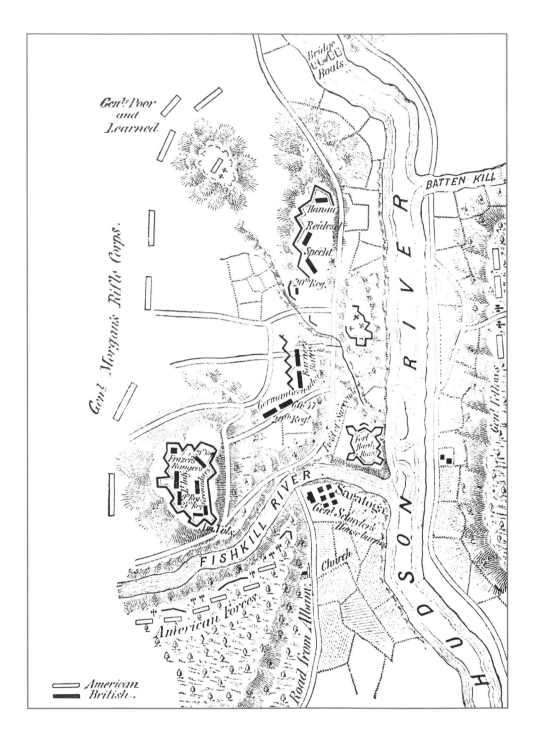

Burgoyne's final position at Saratoga, now known as Schuylerville, was flanked by rebels virtually on all four sides.

SARATOGA

OCTOBER 8, 1777

There was no battle the following day, though snipers took a toll of each other's officers.

Burgoyne tried to be everywhere at once. Like the rest of his men, he had not slept and had eaten little since yesterday morning. More than once he had to calm distraught young officers who demanded an immediate attack. He organized the withdrawal and saw to the disposition of the wounded, the worst of whom would have to be left behind with most of the medical supplies. By now, he knew that his aide, Sir Francis Clarke, had been wounded and captured.

Then there was Simon Fraser's burial.

At sunset, attended by Burgoyne and the staff officers, Fraser's body was carried on a litter up the hill to the grave site. This was a profound moment of sorrow for the entire battered army. The little funeral procession moved in view of both forces, and American cannon began to fire at it. Ignoring the bombardment, the procession bore Fraser to the crest of the hill, with a view of the beautiful countryside and Hudson River in golden autumn. A chaplain read the service while enemy cannonballs bounced around them, scattering dirt, shattering rock. Then the rebel shot stopped striking, although the cannon went on firing, now at one-minute intervals. The Americans had come to realize this was a funeral and now were firing in solemn salute.

Burgoyne's camp after the second battle, seen from the east bank of
the Hudson as Fraser's funeral procession makes its way up the
hillside to his grave site.

Burgoyne wrote about Fraser: "To the canvas and to the faithful page of a more important historian, gallant friend! I consign thy memory. There may thy talents, thy manly virtues, their progress and their period, find due distinction and long may they survive—long after the frail record of my pen shall be forgotten."

It began again to rain.

Before starting the retreat, Burgoyne wrote to Gates, requesting he care for the critically wounded left behind. Then there was one more thing to do on behalf of an officer: Lady Acland's husband also had been wounded and taken prisoner. Determined to go through the lines to be with him, she begged for a pass from Burgoyne.

"I was astonished at this proposal," he later wrote. "After so long an agitation of the spirits, exhausted not only for want of rest, but absolutely want of food, drenched in rains for twelve hours together, that a woman should be capable of such an undertaking as delivering herself to the enemy, probably in the night, and uncertain of what hands she might fall into, appeared an effort above human nature." He reluctantly gave Lady Acland the pass, and she set off with the chaplain as escort.

It continued to rain, a steady downpour that made the retreat slow and agonizing. The narrow, rutted river road was clogged for miles with columns of weary soldiers trying to get past wagons and cannon stuck in the mud as hunger-weakened oxen and horses struggled to pull them free. Hundreds of walking wounded trudged along, and hundreds more lay in rickety carts, some pulled by men. Even the wind was contrary, blowing from the northeast and making it difficult for the boats to get back upriver. It was fortunate Gates did not come in hot pursuit.

Of the original expedition and several hundred reinforcements, fewer than six thousand remained with Burgoyne. Thirteen hundred had been detailed for supply-line garrisons and Ticonderoga; approximately seven hundred had died (among them Clarke, Burgoyne's aide); more than nine hundred were wounded, and eleven hundred were missing. One of the hardest-hit units was

Peters Corps, the Queen's Loyal Rangers, who once had numbered almost three hundred, but now were only ninety. Unlike those loyalists who had joined up after the campaign began, few of these men had deserted.

Above Saratoga, the army again dug in, but there was great confusion and disorganization, owing in part to the loss of so many officers. Rations were held up, and men went hungry. Baron Riedesel's wife used her own provisions to feed as many as thirty starving officers. She angrily summoned Burgoyne to complain that the army had food enough, and it must be issued immediately. Ever courteous, he thanked her for reminding him of his duty.

Burgoyne and his mistress spent that rainy night in General Schuyler's home on the southern bank of the Fishkill. There were those, especially Baroness Riedesel and other Germans, who grumbled to hear the sounds of feasting and of glasses clinking from inside the house while the rest of the army suffered in the cold and wet.

The next day, as the rebels began to come on, and another battle seemed imminent, Burgoyne joined his army across the stream. Since Schuyler's house was blocking the line of fire for Burgoyne's artillery, the place had to be burned down.

There was no new attack, but the riflemen of Daniel Morgan crossed the Fishkill on Burgoyne's right, and before long the turkey call rang out in the forest west of the British encampment. American artillery began to bombard the defenses, and the barrage went on hour after hour, a numbing, wearying curse upon the defenders. Cannonballs bounced on every side, crashing into houses where women and children and wounded were sheltered, one ball bursting in to kill a man who lay on a pallet, undergoing amputation.

On October 12, Burgoyne held another council of war. The weather was still rainy. Rations for only six days were left. The options were, first, to wait for Clinton, who could still be on his way; second, to attack in desperation (angry rank and file were pleading for a wild bayonet charge); third, to retreat across the pontoon bridge with the artillery and baggage; fourth, to abandon everything and hurry back to Fort Edward. Burgoyne wanted the third option, taking the artillery and remaining a fighting force that might yet join with Clinton. The others wanted the fourth option, saving the troops in a dash northward with only pack horses to carry food and ammunition.

At last, Burgoyne gave in and agreed that the army would depart at ten in the evening. He was in a torment of anguish all that day, despising the thought of running away. When just an hour remained before the time of departure, he abruptly canceled the plan to retreat. Overriding the advice of his officers, he said the army would fight on, making its way slowly northward, guns and boats intact. The next morning, however, scouts reported that the river road had been occupied by rebels under John Stark, the victor at Bennington. There was no escape now.

Another war council convened that afternoon, and Burgoyne stood before his staff. He began by saying that he alone was responsible for the situation. Baron Riedesel thanked him for that. Then Burgoyne put the question of capitulation before them. Did they consider it dishonorable under the circumstances? The officers said it was not dishonorable, but added that they and their men would willingly fight to the death if the general required it. As the officers took turns speaking, an American cannonball zoomed close overhead. At the end of the council, the general decided to open negotiations with Gates.

First, Burgoyne distributed part of the military chest to the army, the rest placed in the trust of two Scottish captains who departed on the long journey northward, Burgoyne's mistress going with them. He also allowed the remaining loyalists of Peters Corps to go, for if captured they would be treated harshly by the rebels. They slipped out of camp, vanishing into the forest on trails to Canada.

A truce was declared, and proposal and counterproposal went back and forth between Burgoyne and Gates. Burgoyne insisted the army must have full military honors, all the prisoners to be released after promising never to fight in this war again. They must be sent to Massachusetts, where they would be shipped home as soon as possible. Gates was slow to respond.

Then, on the morning of October 15 Gates surprised Burgoyne by abruptly agreeing to all the terms if only the royal army surrendered at two that afternoon, laying down their arms at five o'clock. Burgoyne became suspicious of Gates's sudden concession, guessing that something had forced his hand. Refusing to be rushed, Burgoyne did not immediately accept the terms. Then he learned Clinton was at last on the move up the Hudson. A loyalist arrived in camp that night to say British forces were at Esopus, about sixty miles below Albany. Gates would have to send troops to meet them, and that was why he was trying to hurry Burgoyne into capitulation.

Burgoyne held another council with his officers and told them the news. They did not want to hear it. They insisted he negotiate in good faith with Gates. Burgoyne tried to change their minds, to make them believe Clinton was coming, but he was alone. The campaign was over. All the general could do to save face was demand that the word "capitulation" not appear on the document of surrender. Instead, the term "convention" was to be used. Further, the grounding of arms was to be done out of sight of the American troops.

Gates accepted, and the ceremonies were set for October 17, a morning that broke sunny and beautiful for the first time in nine days of gloom.

The royal army prepared to surrender with all possible dignity. Officers saw to swords and boots, every uniform made as smart as it could be, though the coats were faded and patched, many stained with blood. The soldiers polished muskets and bayonets for the final time, but some intended to smash them on the ground at the last moment.

There were tears of sorrow and anger in the ranks as Burgoyne, in full regimentals and with a plumed hat, sadly inspected the army. Rather than surrender, many wanted to fight on until they died. Instead, their orders were to march to the ruins of old Fort Hardy near the river, where, unseen by the American army, they would lay down their weapons, regiment by regiment. Then they would parade for the surrender ceremony.

The surrender of Burgoyne's army, depicted in a German sketch, as troops grounded arms on command out of sight of the victorious rebels.

Burgoyne, left, saluted Gates, on white horse, and declares, "The fortune of war, General Gates, has made me your prisoner."

The downcast Burgoyne and his staff rode to the bridge over the Fishkill, where an American led the way to General Gates, a lone horseman waiting in front of his dismounted officers. The two generals, who so long ago had been young lieutenants in the same regiment of foot, drew up their horses, face-to-face. Burgoyne sat upright in the saddle, despite nagging illness and exhaustion; Gates was a squat and undistinguished figure.

Raising his hat, Burgoyne said, "The fortune of war, General Gates, has made me your prisoner."

Gates saluted with his own hat and replied, "I shall always be ready to bear testimony that it has not been through any fault of Your Excellency."

Burgoyne and his staff were invited to a banquet with the American leaders under a large tent. Benedict Arnold had been wounded in the defeat of Breymann and so was not present. Daniel Morgan was there, and Bur-

A nineteenth century view of the Fort Hardy surrender site, where the royal army laid down its arms before marching away as prisoners to Boston.

goyne paid him the compliment of calling his men "the finest regiment of rangers in the world." Gates asked Burgoyne to propose a toast, catching him off guard. After a pause, Burgoyne stood and toasted George Washington. In turn, Gates toasted King George.

Before the formal surrender ceremonies began, Gates's troops formed up on each side of the river road, along which the disarmed royal forces would march with full honors. Burgoyne's officers were impressed by the good discipline of the Americans, whose ranks were straight, their regimental flags and banners emblazoned with patriotic slogans and symbols. As the rebels took their positions, fifers and drummers played brightly, and Burgoyne heard "Yankee Doodle," that old tune once meant to mock Americans. Ever since the rebels had sung and whistled it in their victory at Concord

This woodcut, after the John Trumbull painting, shows Burgoyne
offering his sword to Gates, while the major figures look on,
including Daniel Morgan in white and Philip Schuyler, third from
the right, but not Benedict Arnold, who lay abed, wounded.

and Lexington, "Yankee Doodle" had become a stinging insult to the
British. If the Americans played it when Burgoyne's troops came by, there
surely would be a brawl.

Burgoyne and Gates—one tall and elegant, the other squat and wearing plain clothes—went out of the tent for the surrender. With both armies
arrayed, Burgoyne offered Gates his sword, but the conqueror only touched
the hilt, allowing the conquered the honor of keeping it.

The moment came for the defeated army to pass in review before the
generals. Orders barked out, drums rolled, and each band struck up its
regimental tune. There was no spirit to the music, though, and company
after company marched away from Saratoga. The men were somber, many
crying, as they strode between the American troops, who stood at attention
in solemn and respectful silence.

GENERAL BURGOYNE.

In a portrait published in 1787, five years before his death, John Burgoyne was sixty-four years of age and still a personage of much popular interest in Great Britain

EPILOGUE

John Burgoyne's defeat at Saratoga was the turning point of the American Revolution, for in the wake of the news, France soon declared war against Great Britain. No king's troops ever again marched on Albany, and the British withdrew from the Champlain Valley, abandoning and blowing up Ticonderoga on November 8. Burgoyne's "Convention Army" was kept imprisoned by Congress against the terms of the surrender, not permitted to leave America for years.

In May of 1778, Burgoyne was allowed to return to England to defend his honor against the accusations of enemies. His defeat had been a bitter embarrassment to those in power, and they intended to lay all the blame on him and Howe, even though Colonial Secretary Germain had never sent direct orders for Howe to march north from New York.

Burgoyne demanded a full court-martial to investigate both his conduct and that of the government. He was supported by influential friends in the House of Commons, where debate raged over responsibility for the military catastrophe. His old friend, Charles James Fox, declared in Commons that "the miscarriage of the expedition from Canada was owing to the ignorance and incapacity of the Ministers who planned it and not to the General intrusted with its execution." The court-martial was never allowed, however, because if it had been held, the government's share of the blame would have been all too obvious.

Yet, whoever else was also responsible for the loss of the northern army, Burgoyne's inexperienced generalship and arrogant underestimation of the Americans were instrumental in the disaster. His active military career was over, although he became commander-in-chief of Ireland, a political appointment in recognition of service to the crown. He lived the rest of his years with an Englishwoman he never married, and with whom he had four children. He resumed writing plays, one of his comedies so popular that it was expected to endure long after he died in 1792.

Gentlemanly Johnny Burgoyne's English comedy has been forgotten, but the tragedy he authored in America, with its final tumultuous act at Saratoga, is still very much remembered.

Chapter notes

Chapter 1: St.-Jean, Quebec

It is said that no one can prove the sobriquet "Gentleman Johnny" was ever used during his lifetime. The first published reference is in George Bernard Shaw's 1897 play, *The Devil's Disciple,* wherein Burgoyne is called "Gentlemanly Johnny" by his troops. Hudleston's 1927 biography, entitled Gentleman Johnny Burgoyne, had a considerable role in the popular use of this nickname. Perhaps Hudleston was influenced by Shaw, but since he was employed by the War Office Library in Great Britain, it must be assumed he had extensive knowledge and insight into the published and unpublished history and lore of British military affairs and personalities.

Some of the German auxiliaries were from Hanau, a tiny vassal state ruled by the prince of Hesse-Cassel, whose crown prince was hereditary commander of a Hanau infantry regiment. These troops with Burgoyne—including artillerymen—were referred to as Hesse-Hanauers, but they were not Hessians, nor was there a place called Hesse-Hanau.

Controversy remains over whether the 1777 operations from Canada and New York should be referred to as three-pronged or two-pronged. Since Howe, in New York, never set an advance in motion, and had no intention to, the invasion was two-pronged. Burgoyne, however, and virtually all his army assumed there would be a three-pronged operation, and that Howe would come north in force. King George III himself said "the force from Canada must join [Howe] at Albany," and even George Washington, then in the mid-Atlantic colonies, expected Howe to meet Burgoyne up the Hudson River.

The Burgoyne defeat was a heavy blow to the people in the homelands of his German auxiliaries; within a year, the campaign was memorialized at home by artist F. von Germann, who painted illustrations of soldiers from both the royal and rebel armies.

Chapter 2: The Falls of the Boquet River

The present-day spelling of Boquet River differs from the original "Bouquet" used in 1777; Baxter says the river derives its name from Colonel Henri Bouquet, who was a Swiss officer of high repute serving the British in North America.

Chapter 3: Crown Point, Ticonderoga, and Mount Independence

The actual identity of Burgoyne's French-Canadian mistress is still a mystery, although the great historical novelist Kenneth Roberts refers to her as Marie de Sabrevoir and calls her a spy for Burgoyne. As a side note, there is a town on the Richelieu called Sabrevoir.

Chapter 4: Skenesboro and Fort Anne

The Battle of Hubbardton is being recognized as a crucial engagement in the Revolution, as royal troops met a determined rear guard that stood its ground bravely. Burgoyne's men were given an inkling of what was to come on the open battlefield, where until now they had every expectation of an easy victory.

Chapter 5: Fort Edward

Many explanations for Jane McCrea's death have circulated over the centuries. One claims that she was accidentally shot by a rebel patrol that fired on the party. A century later, when her body was exhumed for reburial, no hatchet marks were found on her skull.

There are those who believe the death of Jane McCrea did not inspire the militias of New England and New York to march against Burgoyne, for they had already been called out. It is also said that the militias' role in the battles of Saratoga—compared with that of the Continental troops—has been overplayed. Yet, Burgoyne rued the fact that he found himself surrounded on all sides by "a rebellious race," including militia, which made communication almost impossible. Later, officers on both sides praised the courage of militia regiments involved in the early engagements and in the climactic battles.

Chapter 6: Fort Miller

Baron Riedesel's memoirs say a provincial who knew the road to Bennington warned Burgoyne that three thousand men were required for the expedition. Thomas Jones, in his history of the loyalists, claims Peters was the provincial mentioned, and the quotes attributed to Peters in this chapter are based on the Jones history. Peters's objections to the expedition as planned are described in correspondence between him and his uncle, a loyalist who had fled to England.

The actual number of Germans at the Battle of Bennington is unclear. Riedesel writes in his memoirs that Lieutenant Colonel Baum commanded five hundred men, composed of the combined Brunswick dragoon and light infantry regiments, a "detachment" of Canadian volunteers, and artillerymen for two cannons. To this, he says, were added one hundred men from Breymann's corps. Jones says rebel Jehu Brown, a prisoner who escaped from Baum, later testified that there were five hundred "Hessians" and about two hundred Canadians in the force.

Popular histories and even paintings often perpetuate a myth by describing the Germans as being heavily equipped, the dragoons with tall fur hats and wearing riding boots. Although Riedesel says the dragoons left Europe "wearing leather pantaloons, high boots, and gauntlets," by the time the 1777 invasion began they had been issued lighter uniforms, much like infantry, and were ready to campaign in a hot, wilderness country.

Chapter 8: Saratoga

Kenneth Roberts says Burgoyne sent his military war chest back to Canada with his mistress and two Scottish officers. Digby's memoirs say Burgoyne distributed the money among the army before the surrender. Probably both happened, with a large part of the cash being sent back to Carleton rather than being allowed to fall into rebel hands.

FOR FURTHER EXPLORATION

Suggested Reading

(Most original texts are also available in modern reprints.)

Anburey, Thomas. *Travels through the Interior Parts of America.* Boston: Houghton Mifflin, 1923.

Anonymous. *Remarks on General Burgoyne's State of the Expedition from Canada.* London: G. Wilkie, 1780.

Atwood, Rodney. *The Hessians.* Cambridge: Cambridge University Press, 1980.

Baxter, James Phinney. *British Invasion from the North, with the Journal of Lieut. William Digby.* New York: Da Capo Press, 1970.

Beach, Allen Penfield. *Lake Champlain as Centuries Pass.* Basin Harbor, Vt.: Basin Harbor Club and Lake Champlain Maritime Museum, 1994.

Bellico, Russell P. *Sails and Steam in the Mountains: A Maritime and Military History of Lake George and Lake Champlain.* Fleischmanns, N.Y.: Purple Mountain Press, 1992.

Bird, Harrison. *March to Saratoga.* New York: Oxford University Press, 1963.

Burgoyne, John. *A State of the Expedition from Canada.* New York: The New York Times and Arno Press, 1969.

Callahan, North. *Royal Raiders.* New York: Bobbs-Merrill, 1963.

Commager, Henry S. and Richard Morris, eds. *The Spirit of Seventy-six.* New York: Harper & Row, 1974.

Cuneo, John R. *The Battles of Saratoga: The Turning of the Tide.* New York: The Macmillan Co., 1967.

DeFonblanque, Edward Barrington. *Political and Military Episodes in the Latter Half of the Eighteenth Century.* London, 1876.

Edgar, Gregory T. *"Liberty or Death!" The Northern Campaigns in the Revolutionary War.* Bowie, Md.: Heritage Books, 1994.

Eelking, Max von, transl. J.G. Rosengarten. *German Allied Troops, 1776-1783*. Albany: Joel Munsell's Sons, 1893.

Elting, John R. *The Battles of Saratoga*. Monmouth Beach, N.J.: Philip Freneau Press, 1977.

Furneaux, Rupert. *The Battles of Saratoga*. New York: Stein and Day, 1971.

Hadden, James Murray. *Hadden's Journal and Orderly Books*. Boston: Gregg Press, 1972.

Hamilton, Edward P. *Fort Ticonderoga: Key to the Continent*. Boston: Little Brown, 1964.

Howson, Gerald. *Burgoyne of Saratoga*. New York: Times Books, 1979.

Hudelston, F.J. *Gentleman Johnny Burgoyne*. Indianapolis: Bobbs- Merrill, 1927.

Jones, Thomas. *History of New York During the Revolutionary War*. 2 Vols. New York, 1879.

Ketchum, Richard M., ed. *The Revolution*. New York: American Heritage Publishing Company, 1958.

Kipping, Ernst. *The Hessian View of America*. Monmouth Beach, N.J.: Philip Freneau Press, 1971.

Lamb, Roger. *An Original and Authentic Journal of Occurrences During the Late American War*. Dublin, Ireland: Wilkinson & Courtney, 1809.

Lancaster, Bruce. *Ticonderoga*. Boston: Houghton Mifflin Co., 1959.

Lord, Philip, Jr. *War Over the Walloomscoick*. Albany: New York State Museum, 1989.

Lossing, Benson J. *The Pictorial Field Book of the Revolution*. 2 vols. New Rochelle: Caratzas Brothers, 1976.

Lowell, Edward J. *The Hessians*. Williamstown, Mass.: Corner House Publishers, 1975.

Lunt, James D. *John Burgoyne of Saratoga*. New York: Harcourt Brace Jovanovich, 1975.

Mintz, Max M. *The Generals of Saratoga*. New Haven & London: Yale University Press, 1990.

Neilson, Charles. *Burgoyne's Invasion, 1777*. Port Washington, N.Y.: Kennikat Press, 1970.

O'Callaghan, E. B., ed. *Orderly Book of Lt. General John Burgoyne from his Entry into the State of New York until his Surrender at Saratoga*. Albany: Joel Munsell, 1860.

Pausch, George. *Journal of Captain Pausch*. William L. Stone, ed. Albany: Joel Munsell's Sons, 1886.

Randall, Willard Sterne. *Benedict Arnold.* New York: Quill, 1990.

Riedesel, Major General Baron Friedrich von. *Memoirs, Letters and Journals.* William L. Stone, translator and ed. Albany: Munsell's Sons, 1868.

Riedesel, Friederike. *Baroness von Riedesel and the American Revolution, Journal and Correspondence of a Tour of Duty 1776-1783.* Ed. Marvin Brown, Jr. Chapel Hill: University of North Carolina Press, 1965.

Roberts, Kenneth. *Rabble in Arms.* Garden City: Doubleday and Company, 1947.

Stanley, George F. G., ed. *For Want of a Horse: Being a Journal of the Campaigns Against the Americans in 1776 and 1777 Conducted by an Officer Who Served with Lieutenant General Burgoyne.* Sackville, New Brunswick: The Tribune Press, 1961.

Stone, William L. *The Campaign of Lieutenant General John Burgoyne, and the Expedition of Lieutenant Colonel Barry St. Leger.* New York: Da Capo Press, 1970.

Stone, William L. *Visits to the Saratoga Battle-grounds, 1780- 1880.* Albany: Joel Munsell's Sons, 1895.

Thacher, James, M.D. *Military Journal During the American Revolutionary War from 1775 to 1783.* Boston: Cottons & Barnard, 1827.

Wilkinson, James. *Memoirs of My Own Times.* Philadelphia, 1816.

Williams, John. *The Battle of Hubbardton.* Montpelier: Vermont Division for Historic Preservation, 1988.

Other Sources

"Orderly Book During Burgoyne's Campaign, 1776/7" kept by Lt. Col. Robert Kingston, chief of staff; courtesy Bennington Museum.

"A Journal of the Carleton and Burgoyne Campaigns," The Bulletin of the Fort Ticonderoga Museum, vol. XI no. 5 (December 1964) pp. 234-269, and no. 6 (September 1965) pp. 307-335; vol. XII no. 1 (March 1966) pp. 4-62.

Fleming, Thomas J. "The Enigma of General Howe." American Heritage, vol. XV, no. 2, (February 1964).

Wallace, Willard M., ed. "The British Occupation of Fort Ticonderoga, 1777," The Bulletin of the Fort Ticonderoga Museum, vol. VIII no. 7 (1951) pp. 301-320.

Wickman, Donald. "Built with Spirit, Deserted in Darkness: The American Occupation of Mount Independence, 1776-1777." MA thesis, University of Vermont, 1993.

Places

Sites on Burgoyne's route and museums with related exhibits listed from north to south:

Fort Chambly, Chambly, Quebec 514-658-1585

Haut-Richelieu Regional Museum and Fort St.-Jean Museum, St.-Jean-sur-Richelieu, Quebec 514-347-0649

Fort Lennox, Ile-aux-Noix, Quebec 514-291-5700

Clinton County Historical Society, Plattsburgh, New York 518-561-0340

Lake Champlain Maritime Museum, Basin Harbor, Vermont 802- 475-2022

Crown Point State Historic Site, Crown Point, New York 518- 597-3666

Fort Ticonderoga, Route 74, Ticonderoga, New York 518-585- 2821

Mount Independence State Historic Site, Orwell, Vermont 802-948-2000

Hubbardton Battlefield State Historic Site, Castleton, Vermont 802-273-2282

Skenesborough Museum, Whitehall, New York 518-499-1155

Old Fort House Museum, Fort Edward, New York 518-747-9600

Bennington Battlefield State Historic Site, Hoosick Falls, New York 518-686-7109

Schuyler House State Historic Site, Schuylerville, New York 518-664-9821

Saratoga National Historical Park, Stillwater, New York 518-664-9821

Saratoga Monument, Schuylerville, New York

Bennington Battle Monument State Historic Site, Bennington, Vermont 802-447-0550

Please contact sites for directions, special events, and schedules, many of which are seasonal.

ACKNOWLEDGMENTS

The author is grateful to all those who kindly contributed their time and expertise to this book. To them goes the credit for what is right, and the author takes responsibility for the rest.

Thanks to William Meuse, former historian at Saratoga National Historical Park, and to staff members Gina Johnson, program director; Paul Okey, historian; Joseph Craig, park ranger; and Jamee Parillo, park ranger; also thanks to Fort Ticonderoga's director, Nicholas Westbrook, and curator, Christopher Fox. Thanks to Audrey Porsche, site administrator for Mount Independence and Hubbardton Battlefield, to Eileen Hannay, education director of the Old Fort House Museum in Fort Edward, and to her associate, Ellen Scott. Thanks to Gregory Furness, historic site manager of Crown Point, to Michael Knapp, site interpreter at Mount Independence, and to Jim Hayden and Mark Nichipor of Eastern National Park & Monument Association. Thanks also to Revolutionary War re-enactors Ron Toelke and Ray Andrews, who were a great help, as were the local history librarians at the Berkshire Athenaeum of Pittsfield, Mass., and the staff of the Chatham Public Library, Chatham, N.Y., and Bennington Museum librarian Tyler Resch.

Thanks to publisher Tordis Ilg Isselhardt for her determination to create the best book possible, to Jan Albers for her helpful suggestions, to book designer Susan Mathews for her patient professionalism, to Don Wickman for sharing his master's thesis on Mount Independence, and to Collins Sennett for her many kindnesses. Thanks to Dr. Roderick Blackburn, Hudson Valley historian, and to John Anson of the New York State Museum for their excellent advice.

Thanks once again, after much too long a spell of not working on the same book, to editor Glenn Novak.

SOURCES OF ILLUSTRATIONS

Cover: Yale University Art Gallery.

X: Copyright, The Frick Collection, New York.

XII, 12, 14, 24, 28, 30, 33, 42, 43, 45, 48, 55, 58, 70, 76, 77, 79, 81, 85, 86, 96, 97: Various sources including *Pictorial Field Book of the Revolution* Vol. II, by Benson J. Lossing, Harper Brothers, New York, 1852.

2-3: National Library of Canada/Bibliothèque nationale du Canada (from Thomas Anburey, *Travels through the interior parts of America,* 1789).

7, 21, 31, 51, 56, 60 (both), 61, 73, 75: Print Collection, Miriam and Ira D. Wallach Division of Art, Prints and Photographs, The New York Public Library, Astor, Lenox and Tilden Foundations (attributed to Friedrich von Germann).

9, 10-11, 18-19, 26-27, 29, 36, 40-41, 52, 88-89, 94, 95, 98: Fort Ticonderoga Museum.

16, 22-23, 82-83: James Hunter (active 1776-1792)/C-001524; James Hunter/ C-001525; Samuel Woodforde (1765-1817)/C-146207 C-020110 ARCHIVES NATIONALES DU CANADA.

66-67: Courtesy of the New York State Museum, Albany, NY.

INDEX

Note: Illustrations are shown in *bold italic* type

IMAGES FROM THE PAST

publishing history in ways that help people see it for themselves

Other Books by Stuart Murray

NORMAN ROCKWELL AT HOME IN VERMONT:
THE ARLINGTON YEARS, 1939–1953

Norman Rockwell's dynamic years in the Vermont village where he painted some of his greatest works. Inspired by the "everyday life of my neighbors," the artist created story-telling pictures that have touched the hearts of millions around the world.

7" x 10"; 96 pages; 13 Rockwell paintings and sketches and 32 historical photographs in black and white; index; regional map, list of area museums, selected bibliography
ISBN 1-884592-02-3 Paperback $14.95

RUDYARD KIPLING IN VERMONT:
BIRTHPLACE OF THE JUNGLE BOOKS

The author's years near Brattleboro, Vermont (1892-96) where he and his American wife built a home and had two children, and Kipling wrote some of his most acclaimed works. He loved Vermont and wanted to stay there, but due to Kipling's feud with his brother-in-law that resulted in embarrassing publicity, the author left America forever.

6" x 9" 198 pages; 21 historical photos; 6 book illustrations and 7 sketches; index
ISBN 1-884592-04-X Hardcover $29.00
ISBN 1-884592-05-8 Paperback $18.95

Other Images from the Past titles you might enjoy:

BENNINGTON'S BATTLE MONUMENT:
MASSIVE AND LOFTY
by Tyler Resch

Design and construction (modern text and contemporary newspaper articles) of the 306'
dolomite tower dedicated in 1891 to commemorate the Revolutionary War victory
which presaged Burgoyne's surrender at Saratoga.

7" x11"; 64 pages; modern and historic photos; portraits of Presidents Hayes and Harrison; sketches of rejected designs; birdseye view of the town in 1887
ISBN 1-884592-00-7 Paperback $9.95

REMEMBERING GRANDMA MOSES
by Beth Moses Hickok

Set in 1934, this is a portrayal, not of Grandma Moses's primitive paintings, but the
woman herself: a crusty, feisty, upstate New York farm wife and grandmother, as remembered in affectionate detail from letters and diaries by Beth Moses Hickok, who
married into the family at 22, and raised two of Grandma's granddaughters.

6" x 9"; 64 pages; portraits of Grandma Moses from 1947 and 1949, 9 historical photos and 9 contemporary photos in black and white
ISBN 1-884592-01-5 Paperback: $12.95

ALLIGATORS ALWAYS DRESS FOR DINNER:
AN ALPHABET BOOK OF VINTAGE PHOTOGRAPHS
by Linda Donigan and Michael Horwitz

Late 19th and early 20th century images reproduced in sepia duotone for children and
collectors. Each two-page spread offers a surprising visual treat.
9 1/4" x 9 3/4"; 64 pages; 28 duotone photos; A-Z info pages with image details
ISBN 1-884592-08-2 Hardcover: $25.00

Available through your local bookstore or from Images from the Past, Inc.,

Box 137 Bennington, Vermont 05201 (888) 442-3204

When ordering, please add $3.50 shipping and handling for the first book and $1 for
each additional. Add 5% sales tax for shipments to Vermont.